Handmade Christmas

Handmade Christmas

the best of martha stewart living

The recipes and photographs in this work were previously published in MARTHA STEWART LIVING.

Manufactured in the United States of America.
Library of Congress Catalog Number: 95-69966
ISBN: 0-8487-14776 (hardcover)
0-8487-1475-X (paperback)

EDITORS: Susan Wyland, Evelyn Renold, Amy Schuler
DESIGN ASSOCIATES: Arlene Gertzulin, Marcel Sarmiento

ENDPAPER PHOTOGRAPHY: Don Freeman

DESIGN: Laura Harrigan, Art Director of Special Projects
Martha Stewart Living

ACKNOWLEDGEMENTS

Many, many people have contributed to the issues of MARTHA STEWART LIVING from which this book is drawn.

From the magazine: David Steward, Gael Towey, Susan Wyland, Isolde Motley, Peter Mark, Sarah Medford, Linda Nardi, Lisa Wagner, Wayne Wolf, Peter Herbert, Tamara Westmark, Carol Kramer, Susan Spungen, Hannah Milman, Tamara Glenny, Eugenia Leftwich, Lauren Stanich, Laurel Reed Caputo, Eric Pike, Wanda Lau, Celia Barbour, Anne Johnson, Darcy Miller, Dora Braschi Cardinale, Marc Einsele, George Planding, Heidi Posner, Christina Frederick, Lillian Fuentes, Carole Rogers, Frances Boswell, Jane Yagoda, Susan Sugarman, William L. Hamilton, Ingrid Abramovitch, Stephen Earle, Claudia Bruno, Lyn Ringer, Page Marchese, Pete Curtner, Paula Blum, Heidi Petelinz, and Eric Handman.

From Martha's home and in her Westport office: Renato Abreu, Rita Christiansen, Necy Fernandes, Carolyn Kelly, Marie Mendez, Judy Morris, Kathleen Oberman, Laura Herbert Plimpton, and Alexis Stewart.

From Oxmoor House, in Birmingham, Alabama: Bruce Akin, Nancy Fitzpatrick, Marianne Jordan, Phillip Lee, John McIntosh, and Gail Morris. From Satellite Graphics, in New York City, Ernest V. Cardinale, and from Quebecor Printing, in Kingsport, Tennessee, Myra Tiller and Linda Campbell.

For their inspiration and support: Aimee Lee Ball, Jerry Bolduan, Lisa Bradkin, Diana Burke, Anita Calero, Julia Claiborne Johnson, Fritz Karch, Brad Kessler, O'Hara Mars, Jeffrey W. Miller, Deborah Smith Morant, Ayesha Patel, Bernard Roth, Steve Rubin, Mary Talbot, and Robert Valentine.

CONTENTS

INTRODUCTION

Of all the holidays we celebrate, Christmas is by far the most "hands on." The image of Santa's little helpers conveys a sense of industry that no other holiday comes close to approximating. The literature of the season evokes homes filled with fragrant aromas of baking and cooking; stories tell of gift-giving and gift-making; biblical references remind us of church-going and special religious observances; and television is full of movies and programs befitting this season of hustle and bustle.

My own Christmas traditions have always incorporated homemade things, and for as long as I can remember I have found that Christmas inspires tremendous variety when it comes to handmade gifts, decorations, and food.

For my family, Christmas begins in earnest right after Thanksgiving. Of course, all year long I am on the lookout for a new color combination for Christmas, the perfect ribbons, the best idea for decorating the trees, and for general inspiration. Indeed, inspiration is the key to making the Christmas season and its celebrations memorable. On a recent trip to San Francisco, I discovered wonderful velvet and silk ribbons in unexpected colors that I know will garland my halls and chandeliers this Christmas. They will help me create a very different look from last year, when the house was swagged with pine branches and chartreuse ribbons. Whether it comes in the form of a color scheme, a recipe, or a newly discovered carol or prayer or story, inspiration is what makes the holiday season fun and, most importantly, meaningful.

My first task is to chop the fruit and nuts for my traditional plum puddings, fruitcakes, and panettones that I bake for gift-giving in paper bags. I mix up batches of cookie dough, starting with the shortbread and sugar cookies, which taste better when baked weeks before Christmas. I like to sew something special for my closest friends, and I have made many silk-lined scarves, oversized aprons, and beautiful napkins and tablecloths for them in the last few years. For the children in my life, I always make special gifts. My niece Sophie, who is eleven, loves projects, so she gets a homemade craft kit with which she can make something herself. My godson Kirk, also aged eleven, loves the outdoors, so his gift reflects that interest in a how-to project. My daughter, Alexis, dotes on her English bulldogs, so special sweaters or booties or homemade dog beds are de rigueur.

This book, which brings together the best holiday ideas from the last four years of MARTHA STEWART LIVING, has many of my favorite ideas for making Christmas a very special time of year. My editors and I have gathered projects that we think are both unique and doable. Wherever possible, we have included the sources from which you can obtain the same materials we used. I know that you and your family will enjoy these projects, and I hope that you will use this book for years to come.

Martha Stewart

WREATHS & SWAGS

A sure harbinger of the holidays, these adornments are as welcoming as they are festive

Unlike other Christmas items—ornaments, trees, stockings—

a wreath is self-contained; it needs nothing but itself and can go virtually

anywhere, on doors, walls and tabletops, indoors or out.

We are endlessly fascinated by wreaths, by their shape and texture and the smell

of their foliage, still green and fragrant from the field where they were cut.

A wreath is a circle completing itself, an animal curled tightly in a ball.

It has no beginning, middle, or end. It is a world of its own, as complete as a globe.

And yet, wreaths need not come in circles. They may be built in squares, triangles, sheathes,

swags, ropes, and garlands. And they need not be made of fir or pine or spruce. They should

reflect the diversity of the North American landscape and employ whatever is local.

They may be twined with toyon or redwood on the California coast; dried chile peppers in Louisiana;

succulents or sage in the Southwest. They may be wrought with sycamore seed

cases in New York City or with moss in the rain forests of the Cascades.

Either way, a wreath, like a ring or a ribbon

around a tree, is a reminder and a promise kept,

as welcoming as a front doormat.

OPPOSITE: A white-pine garland (below left) is draped over a railing, while a viburnum-berry wreath (above right) rests in front of a mirror.

THIS PAGE: Many wreaths fall halfway between shrub and decoration, with a friendly shagginess about them. But this one is elegant enough for the finest parlor. Made with pale eucalyptus leaves and a large silver bow, it will keep for several seasons. (See page 16 for instructions.)

JUNIPER

BOXWOOD

BOXWOOD

JUNIPER

HOLLY

HINOKI FALSE CYPRESS

SHORE JUNIPER

BIRDFOOT

SHORE JUNIPER

LEAVES AND BRANCHES

Not to disparage the hardy evergreen, but inspiration for holiday decoration can be found elsewhere. Using different leaves and berries, you can incorporate a whole range of natural colors, scents, shapes, and textures that often get lost in the Christmas shuffle.

LEFT: A silver-painted laurel wreath hangs, halolike, on a doorknob, as though left by an off-duty angel.

BELOW LEFT: Fresh viburnum leaves are sewn together to make a swag that's wrapped around a classic column.

BELOW: The hanging oak-leaf wreath incorporates some three hundred leaves gathered after they had turned gold. The sphere-shaped wreath, inspired by the geometry of topiary, was made of fresh plum twigs secured by floral wire.

TECHNIQUES

By definition, a wreath is something twisted into a round form. But wreaths can be just as attractive in rectangles, diamonds, and ovals. Buy ready-made forms, or clip and shape wreath wire from a flower shop or craft-supply store into whatever shape you like, securing the joints with florist's wire.

basic procedure (1)

Using green floral wire, bind little bunches of conifer, boxwood, or other material into sprigs (cut them from your own shrubs, if possible). Wrap wire around the sprigs' stems and then twist the ends around the wreath frame. Affix each piece of greenery individually, or use one piece of wire to bind your sprigs to the frame in a series of loops.

eucalyptus wreath (2)

To make the wreath on page 13, strip about 80 mature eucalyptus leaves from their branches, layer them between sheets of wax paper, and press them overnight beneath a stack of books. They have a natural curve to their stems; select an equal number of left-leaning and right-leaning leaves. Bind

them one at a time to a 10"-diameter wreath frame with a single length of floral wire, coiling it several times around each stem before placing the next leaf on the frame overlapping the previous stem. To finish, loop through 2 yards of 2"-wide ribbon and tie in a big bow.

oak-leaf wreath (3)

Following the basic wreath-building technique described above, create small bunches of leaves, flatten on one side, and wire one after another to an 18" double flat wreath form. By using leaves gathered while they were still on the branch (rather than on the ground), you get a much fuller wreath, with realistic variations in leaf size.

flowering-plum sphere (4)

The sphere is built on a 10" grapevine armature. Wire together small bunches of flowering plum or other stiff and hardy leafy twigs, such as boxwood, oak, or snowberry. Poke bunched stems into center of the armature and wire stems to vines to cover the form. (To make an armature in another geometric shape, wire together supple branches with chicken wire or a metal wreath form.)

viburnum swag (5)

This swag is best used as a more temporary decoration, such as for a holiday open house or dinner party. It is essential to use fresh leaves, as they will start to curl as they dry and will not lie flat. Sew leaves together above the stem with cotton thread (we chose a green that blended with the leaves), layering them snugly atop each other. Drape the swag around a column, across a mantelpiece, or on a wall.

topiary trees

You don't have to limit yourself to just one large Christmas tree. With diminutive topiaries (below), you can have an evergreen forest on a mantel, tabletop, or windowsill. Use any tiny receptacle, from a small clay pot to an antique egg cup, as a base. The topiaries also make great gifts for someone who doesn't have room for a big tree.

To make the topiaries, cut off tips from holly, boxwood, or conifers such as cedar, spruce, juniper, or pine. Cut these into sprigs, slicing the stems at an angle as you would flowers. Then, using florist's wire, attach sprigs to two-inch wooden flower picks. Carve green floral foam (available at any florist or garden-supply store) that has been soaked in water overnight into a cone, light-bulb, or brick shape. Encase in chicken wire to prevent crumbling and press into a small pot or cup. Then push the wrapped picks into the form until it's covered, making sure the plant stems penetrate the foam. Use U-shaped pins to secure unruly sprigs. Keep the foam well watered and out of direct sunlight so your topiaries last throughout the holidays. Some varieties will stay green even after they've dried.

moss balls

Moss balls are the earthiest of Christmas decorations. Yet they can look very elegant as part of a centerpiece on a holiday table. With daily misting, the moss will stay fresh for weeks.

1. Soak sheet moss in water until pliable; squeeze out excess.

2, 3. Wrap Styrofoam forms with moss as you would a package, covering surface completely. Secure with florist's U pins.

4. Natural accents can be wired to finished balls: try grape or bittersweet vine, ivy, berries, or blossoms.

SUCCULENT WREATH

Succulents are those fascinating plants that often look like stones, babies' toes, or the old-fashioned cloth flowers used for hat decorations. They are essential elements in the drought-tolerant garden. Some of the better-known succulents include the ubiquitous hen-and-chickens *(Sempervivum tectorum)*, the beautiful but ill-used jade tree *(Crassula argentea)*, and the aloe of burn-soothing fame. Succulent wreaths look good, indoors and out, not only at Christmas, but in all seasons. With proper care, a wreath will last for years.

Teddy Colbert, a Los Angeles-based gardener and writer, has a thriving business selling ready-made wreaths and swags as well as the frames, hardware, bases, cuttings, and accessories needed to create succulent decorations.

Although you can improvise a wreath from found materials, it is more efficient to order a kit from Colbert: you will need at least two hundred cuttings (see The Guide). Cuttings should be two to three inches long, the bottom inch free of leaves. Spread in a single layer on a tray and keep dry. In a day to a week, calluses will form over cut ends; new roots will sprout along the stems. (If a cutting is planted before a callus forms, or if it gets wet, the plant will rot, not root.)

To prepare, soak a one-inch-thick mat of sphagnum moss, three times the diameter of frame, in water overnight and drain well. Lay moss "good" side down; place frame on top. Insert two S hooks into frame's crossbar.

1. Cover the frame with moist soil.
2. Fold moss around frame and secure by wrapping with a length of copper wire. (It is best if two people work together on this.)
3, 4. To plant, make holes with a pencil point and insert callused ends of cuttings. Press moss around stems, and, if necessary, secure with fern pins.
5. As the wreath gets fuller, tweezers and forceps make planting easier, allowing for more precise placement of plants.
6. Fill in any bare spots in the wreath with additional succulents.

Allow wreath to rest in a horizontal position for about two weeks. Attach ends of a sturdy chain to S hooks; pull a third hook through middle of chain and hang. Do not water your wreath if moss is dry on the outside but soft on the inside, like fresh bread. If inside is firm, like stale bread, water deeply. Never mist: This encourages roots to move near the surface, where they will dry out.

This mature living wreath is composed of twenty kinds of succulents. The wreath can be hung outdoors—except, of course, when there is a danger of frost.

DECORATING
WITH ORNAMENTS

OPPOSITE: Deep-green laurel leaves are dusted with silver and punctuated with glass balls in the garland. A wreath (above right) can also be made from the same materials, and attached to a frame as described on page 16.

To make the garland, begin with 1 to 2 pounds of laurel, available from flower shops. Tear off leaf clusters by the stem. Spray leaves with silver floral paint, giving half the clusters a solid coat and half a light spritz. Prepare 60 silver balls, ½" to 1" in diameter, by bending tips of pipe cleaners into hooks and poking one into the hole in each ball (above). Gather balls into twos and threes, wrapping stems together with green florist's tape. Cut a piece of green twine to desired length of finished garland (right). Bind stem of a spritzed leaf cluster to twine with floral wire. Add a silvered cluster 1" farther along, wrapping wire around stems and twine. Continue binding alternating clusters, adding balls every 4 to 6 inches. When one side and top length of garland are completed, begin again from other end.

grape ornaments

THIS PAGE: You can borrow one of nature's prettiest designs and make bunches of grapes out of tiny glass ornaments. You'll need 25 glass balls ranging in size from ⅝" to 1" for each bunch. Remove the wire hanger from one ⅝" ball. Fold the tip of a pipe cleaner into a hook and poke it into the opening, so that it catches inside the ball and holds it securely. String the remaining balls on the pipe cleaner by their wire hangers (above), increasing the size as you go. Make a tendril (below left) by coiling another piece of pipe cleaner around a nail. Twist the tendril, together with a fabric leaf, to pipe-cleaner stem to finish the cluster.

clustered glass balls

OPPOSITE: Renew small, faded glass Christmas balls by stringing three or four together on a strand of wire and adding a few decorative leaves. These have been hung from a spiraling garland of ivy, but they can also be used as tree ornaments.

BERRIES

Berries are customarily used as accents in holiday decorations, but they can make striking wreaths all by themselves. This square wreath uses sprigs of holly berries.

LEFT: A wreath of viburnum berries and crab apples can last a month if berries are chosen when small and hard.

BELOW LEFT: To make a berry wreath, wrap floral wire around berry sprigs' stems and then twist ends around wreath frames. The diamond-shaped wreath is made from juniper.

BELOW: Pepperberry is available from many florists during winter months. To make a pepperberry tree, mount a Styrofoam cone on a wooden "stem" and secure in a pot filled with floral foam. (Styrofoam cones come in a variety of sizes, and you can find a wooden dowel to accommodate the size you choose.) Use floral wire to attach sheet moss to cone; hot-glue pepperberry sprigs to moss, starting at top and working until moss is barely visible. Keep tree out of direct sun; berries can fade.

OPPOSITE: A fresh rose-hip wreath frames a family portrait on the mantel.

THIS PAGE: A pomegranate-and-viburnum-berry wreath hangs on the door, with a white-pine swag overhead and tassels of pine and berries suspended from the lamps.

COOKIE BOXES

Unexpected containers enhance the appeal of the most delicious and ubiquitous of Christmas gifts

The only thing we liked better than Christmas cookies were the boxes they came in.

Whether as humble as cardboard or hammered from ornate tin,

cookie boxes were exciting, because they hinted strongly of the

holiday to come. Just thinking about what was inside made the mouth water.

Cookies last only a few days, but a cookie box will last a lifetime. It should not be given

short shrift, for after the cookies are gone it can become a container for pens and

pencils, a kitchen ornament, a spice box, a vessel for fresh flowers. A cookie box will always

remind us of what it once contained—the almond crisps and pecan sandies,

shortcake and sugar cookies that enveloped the season in sweetness.

OPPOSITE: An 8"-square baking tin is lined with parchment paper and decorated with military ribbon.

THIS PAGE: Ice-cream molds can be used well after the Christmas season. This one has a band of military ribbon and gold rickrack glued at the edge with fabric adhesive. A gauzy silver ribbon holds the sugar cookies in place.

Almost any tin with an interesting shape can make an attractive gift container for Christmas cookies. Pudding molds in half-moon forms can be found at kitchen-supply stores. The lidded mold was tied with moiré ribbon; colored waxed paper covers the other, tied with bookbinder's tape.

For Emma

almond crisps

makes 4 to 5 dozen

Nonstick cooking spray
9½ ounces unblanched almonds,
finely ground (2½ cups finely ground)
1½ cups sugar
3 large egg whites
1 teaspoon almond extract
1 teaspoon vanilla extract
½ cup unblanched almond slices

1. Heat oven to 375°. Line a baking
sheet with parchment and lightly coat with
nonstick cooking spray. In the bowl of an
electric mixer fitted with the paddle attachment, combine ground almonds, sugar, and
egg whites. Beat on medium speed until
thick, about 3 minutes. Beat in extracts.
2. With dampened hands, roll dough into
1-inch balls and place 2 inches apart on prepared baking sheet. Flatten each ball with
fingers; gently press 2 sliced almonds on top.
3. Bake until just brown on top, about 10
minutes. Remove from oven and place on a
wire rack for 5 to 10 minutes. Remove
cookies from baking sheet while still warm
and place on a wire rack to cool.

pecan sandies

makes about 5 dozen

½ pound (2 sticks) unsalted butter
⅓ cup granulated sugar
1 teaspoon vanilla extract
⅔ cup pecans, finely ground
1⅔ cup all-purpose flour
Pinch of salt
¼ cup confectioners' sugar

1. Heat oven to 350°. In the bowl of an
electric mixer, beat butter and sugar with the
paddle attachment on medium-high speed
until light and creamy, about 3 minutes.
Beat in vanilla.
2. Mix the ground pecans with the flour
and salt and add to butter mixture. Beat,
beginning on low speed and increasing
to medium, until combined, about 1 minute.
3. Lightly flour palms, if necessary, and
roll dough into ¾-inch balls. Place on an
ungreased baking sheet 1 inch apart. Bake
until just brown on edges, 20 to 25 minutes.
Remove cookies from baking sheet while
they are still warm, and lightly sift confectioners' sugar over tops.

BELOW: Christmas cookies of different sizes,
shapes, and textures nestle in a heavy-duty
cake pan. Round sugar cookies are tied with
jute string, tree-shaped cookies with braided
straw. Edible gold dust and dragées—small,
round sugar decorations that look like miniature ornaments—were sprinkled on the tree-
shaped cookies. Fluted cupcake liners are
repositories for shortbread wedges, almond
crisps, pecan sandies, and Linzer cookies.

chocolate armagnac truffles
makes 5 dozen

- 12 ounces semisweet good-quality chocolate, such as Lindt or Ghirardelli
- ½ cup heavy cream
- 2 tablespoons Armagnac (brandy or orange liqueur may be substituted)
- ½ cup Dutch-processed unsweetened cocoa, sifted

1. Chop chocolate and place in a bowl. Bring cream to a boil in a small, heavy saucepan; pour over chocolate. Let stand for 5 minutes; stir until smooth. Stir in liqueur. Refrigerate until firm, at least 3 hours or overnight.
2. Scoop up ½ teaspoon of chilled chocolate and quickly roll into a ball. Continue until mixture is used up. Roll each truffle in cocoa to coat. Chill until firm. Store in an airtight container in the refrigerator for up to 2 weeks.

almond lace cookies
makes 30

These cookies can be left flat or rolled into cones or cylinders. They can also be dipped in chocolate.

- 4 tablespoons unsalted butter
- 2 tablespoons heavy cream
- 1 tablespoon orange liqueur
- ¾ cup whole unblanched almonds, ground medium fine
- 1 tablespoon all-purpose flour
- ½ cup sugar

1. Heat oven to 375°. Line a baking sheet with parchment. In a small saucepan over medium heat, combine butter, cream, and orange liqueur. When butter has melted, stir in remaining ingredients with a wooden spoon. Cook until gently bubbling, 2 to 3 minutes. Remove from heat and keep warm.
2. Place 5 half teaspoons of batter 1½ inches apart on prepared baking sheet (this is as many as you can mold while hot). Bake until lightly browned and crisp, 6 to 7 minutes.
3. Remove from oven and let sit for 1 to 2 minutes. Working quickly, lay each cookie over a cone-shaped object (we used a water-cooler cup), pressing edges together. Alternatively, roll cookies around the handle of a wooden spoon, pressing the edges together to form a cylinder. Continue baking and forming cookies until batter is used up. Place cookies on a wire rack to cool.

coconut pyramids
makes 45

These macaroons work best with unsweetened coconut, but if you can't find it, use the variation for sweetened coconut.

- 1¾ cups sugar
- 5¼ cups unsweetened shredded coconut (see "The Guide" for sources)
- 7 large egg whites
  Pinch of salt
- 2 tablespoons unsalted butter, melted
- 1 teaspoon almond extract
- 1 teaspoon vanilla extract
- 4 ounces semisweet chocolate
- ½ teaspoon vegetable shortening

1. Heat oven to 350°. Line a baking sheet with parchment. In a large bowl, using your hands, mix together sugar, coconut, egg whites, and salt. Add butter and extracts and combine well. Refrigerate for at least 1 hour.
2. Moisten palms of hands with cold water. Roll 1 tablespoon of the coconut mixture in palms, squeezing tightly together 2 or 3 times to form a compact ball. Place ball on a clean surface and, using a spatula, flatten one side at a time to form a pyramid shape.
3. Place pyramids on the prepared baking sheet about 1 inch apart and bake until edges are golden brown, about 15 minutes. Cool completely on baking sheet on a wire rack.
4. Place chocolate and shortening in a small heatproof bowl and set over a pan of simmering water; stir occasionally until melted. Dip top ½ inch of each pyramid in the melted chocolate. Set each dipped macaroon on cooled baking sheet to allow chocolate to harden.

SWEETENED COCONUT VARIATION: Substitute ½ cup sugar, 4 cups sweetened coconut, 3 large egg whites, ½ teaspoon almond extract, and ½ teaspoon vanilla extract. Recipe steps and amounts of other ingredients remain the same.

shortbread wedges
makes 3 dozen

- 1 pound (4 sticks) unsalted butter
- 1 cup firmly packed light brown sugar
- 5 cups all-purpose flour
- 1 teaspoon salt
- 1 teaspoon vanilla extract

1. Heat oven to 275°. Grease three 8-inch springform pans. In the bowl of an electric mixer, beat butter and sugar on medium-high speed until light and creamy, about 2 minutes. Add flour, salt, and vanilla and mix, beginning on low speed and increasing to medium, until flour is just combined.
2. Divide dough evenly among prepared pans. Using a spatula, spread dough out to edges, making sure the tops are smooth and level.
3. Lightly score dough in each pan into 12 equal wedges. Prick a pattern into each wedge with the tines of a fork. Bake until shortbread is dry and barely golden, about 50 minutes. Cool on a wire rack. Using a sharp knife, follow the score marks to cut into neat wedges.

THIS PAGE: The almond lace cookies (far left) were rolled while warm into cornets, while the coconut macaroons were hand-molded into pyramid shapes and tipped with chocolate.

OPPOSITE: A fluted pudding mold is filled with chocolate Armagnac truffles. The center stem as well as the sides of the mold are lined with parchment paper cut to fit.

linzer cookies
makes about 5 dozen

- ½ pound (2 sticks) unsalted butter
- ⅔ cup sugar
- 2 large eggs
- 1 teaspoon vanilla extract
- 2 cups all-purpose flour
- 1 teaspoon baking powder
- 1 teaspoon cinnamon
- ¼ teaspoon salt
- 1 teaspoon lemon zest
- 1¼ cup hazelnuts, ground medium fine
- ½ cup seedless raspberry or cherry jam

1. Heat oven to 350°. In the bowl of an electric mixer, beat butter and sugar at medium-high speed until light and creamy, about 2 minutes. Add eggs and beat until smooth, about 3 minutes. Beat in vanilla.
2. Combine flour, baking powder, cinnamon, salt, and zest. Add to butter mixture; beat on medium speed until combined, about 1 minute. Refrigerate for at least 30 minutes.
3. Form dough into ¾-inch balls and roll in ground hazelnuts. Place balls on ungreased baking sheet 1 inch apart. Bake until cookies begin to set, about 8 minutes. Remove from oven. Working quickly, make a slight indentation in each cookie with your thumb. Return to oven and bake about 8 minutes more. Place on a wire rack to cool. When cool enough to handle, transfer cookies to rack.
4. Melt the jam in a small saucepan over medium-low heat. Place ¼ to ½ teaspoon of jam in each indentation. Cool completely.

OPPOSITE: Three different ice-cream molds perch atop a paint box, found at an art-supply store. A pipe-cleaner handle, antique ribbon, and bookbinder's headband tape add special touches. The paint-box handle is tied with seam binding from a notions counter.

THIS PAGE: Fabric ribbon is woven through the crevices of a baking mold (background) and a brioche mold, creating a star-shaped effect.

pistachio-fig biscotti
makes 3 dozen

These crunchy Italian cookies are delicious dipped in coffee or dessert wine.

- ½ teaspoon fennel seeds
- 8 tablespoons (1 stick) unsalted butter
- ¾ cup sugar
- 2 large eggs
- 1 teaspoon vanilla extract
- 1 teaspoon anise extract or Sambuca
- 1 teaspoon lemon zest
- 2¼ cups all-purpose flour
- 1½ teaspoons baking powder
- ¼ teaspoon salt
- ½ cup shelled pistachios
- 4 ounces dried figs (about 6 large), stems removed, cut into ¼-inch dice

1. Heat oven to 350°. In a small pan over medium-low heat, toast the fennel seeds, swirling the pan; set aside. In the bowl of an electric mixer, beat butter and sugar on medium-high speed with paddle attachment until smooth, about 2 minutes. Add eggs, extracts, and zest and beat on medium speed until creamy and light, 2 to 3 minutes.
2. In a medium bowl, combine remaining ingredients and add to butter mixture. Mix on low speed until just incorporated. Remove dough to a clean surface and divide into quarters. Form into 9-by-1-inch logs, place on an ungreased baking sheet 2 inches apart, and bake until lightly browned, 25 to 30 minutes.
3. Remove baking sheet from oven and let logs cool slightly. Lower oven temperature to 275°. Using a serrated knife, slice logs on the diagonal about ½ inch thick. Arrange biscotti on their sides on baking sheet. Return to oven and bake until golden, about 30 minutes. Turn biscotti over and bake for 30 minutes more.

ABOVE: A long, narrow Pullman bread pan is a perfect container for pistachio-fig biscotti.

RIGHT: The lidded bread pans contain almond crisps. The pan on top is wrapped with a strip of chartreuse antique taffeta, the bottom with an indigo-blue ribbon and antique silver cord.

These heavy-duty square cake pans have notched corners, which are perfect for securing the twenty-five-cents-a-yard rickrack that crisscrosses over the parchment-paper lids.

chocolate thumbprints

makes 2 dozen

- 12 tablespoons (1½ sticks) unsalted butter
- ½ cup confectioners' sugar
- ¼ teaspoon salt
- 1 teaspoon vanilla extract
- 1¼ cups all-purpose flour
- 4 ounces semisweet chocolate, chopped
- 1½ teaspoons corn syrup

1. Heat oven to 350°. In the bowl of an electric mixer, beat together 1 stick butter, sugar, salt, and vanilla on medium-high speed with paddle attachment until smooth, about 2 minutes. Beat in flour, beginning on low speed and increasing to medium high.
2. Roll dough by teaspoonfuls into balls and place 1 inch apart on an ungreased baking sheet. Bake for 10 minutes, remove from oven, and press thumb into tops of cookies to make indentations. Return to oven and bake until light brown on the edges, 7 to 9 minutes more. Remove to a wire rack to cool.
3. Combine chocolate, 4 tablespoons butter, and corn syrup in a small heatproof bowl. Set over a pot of simmering water; stir occasionally until melted and smooth. Allow to cool slightly. When cookies are cool, fill the thumbprints with the chocolate mixture.

sugar cookies

makes 7 dozen small or 2 dozen large cookies

- ½ pound (2 sticks) unsalted butter
- ¾ cup sugar
- 2 large egg yolks
- 1 teaspoon vanilla extract
- 1 tablespoon orange liqueur or cognac
- 2½ cups all-purpose flour
- 1½ teaspoons baking powder
  Pinch of salt
- 1 large egg yolk mixed with 1 tablespoon heavy cream, for egg wash
- 3 tablespoons sugar, for sprinkling

1. Heat oven to 350°. Line a baking sheet with parchment. In the bowl of an electric mixer, beat butter and sugar on medium-high speed until smooth, about 2 minutes.

OPPOSITE: The paint box contains raisin bars, Linzer cookies, chocolate thumbprints, almond lace cookies, sugar cookies in tree and star shapes, pecan sandies, and chocolate truffles.

THIS PAGE: Raisin bars, cut into pieces.

Add yolks and beat until fluffy, 2 to 3 minutes. Beat in vanilla and liqueur. Add flour, baking powder, and salt and mix, beginning on low speed and increasing to medium, until flour is just incorporated.
2. Turn dough out onto a clean surface and divide evenly into 2 portions. Flatten each half to a 1-inch-thick disk, wrap in plastic, and refrigerate for at least 1 hour.
3. Lightly flour a clean surface. Roll dough to ¼ inch thick and cut into shapes. Decorate as desired, brush with egg wash, or sprinkle with sugar. (Scraps can be combined and rolled one more time.) Bake until golden, 10 to 15 minutes. Remove cookies to a wire rack to cool.

raisin bars

makes 2 dozen

- 1 recipe sugar-cookie dough (see above)
- 2 cups raisins
- ½ cup pure maple syrup
- ⅓ cup orange juice
- 1½ teaspoons orange zest
- 1 tablespoon all-purpose flour
- 1 large egg yolk mixed with 1 tablespoon heavy cream, for egg wash

1. Make cookie dough and form into 2 disks; chill for at least 30 minutes.
2. Combine raisins, syrup, juice, zest, and flour in a heavy saucepan. Bring to a boil over medium-low heat and cook until mixture thickens and raisins are plumped, 4 to 5 minutes. Remove from heat and let cool slightly. Place in a food processor and pulse until almost pureed.
3. Cut disks of cookie dough in half; roll each half into a 9-by-6-inch rectangle, ¼-inch thick. Refrigerate for at least 20 minutes.
4. Place 1 dough rectangle on a lightly floured surface. Cut in half lengthwise. Lightly score one piece crosswise at 1½-inch intervals. Place 3 tablespoons raisin mixture on the unscored rectangle; spread evenly to ¼ inch from the edges. Using 2 large spatulas, lift the scored half and carefully place on top. Repeat this process three times more with the remaining dough, placing each completed bar in refrigerator until ready to bake.
5. Brush bars with egg wash. Bake until golden brown, about 20 minutes. Remove to a wire rack to cool. Use a sharp knife to cut the bars along the score marks into 6 pieces.

VARIATION FOR ORANGE MARMALADE COOKIES: Substitute ¾ cup orange marmalade for the raisin mixture.

COOKIE TIPS

1. In choosing recipes, bear in mind that some cookies keep better than others. Cookies don't turn bad—they just lose whatever texture they have: Crunchy goes soggy, soft gets hard. Shortbread, for example, is sturdier than a traditional butter cookie because it has no eggs; a spongy biscotti can be thrown back in the oven to dry out a bit.

2. You can safely double most recipes, but don't try further multiples. Creaming or beating sugar and eggs thoroughly requires incorporating a lot of air, which you can't do with a big batter in a small mixer.

3. Before you bake, borrow lots of cookie sheets and spray them with vegetable oil, which is faster than buttering, or use parchment paper so you won't need to keep cleaning and reoiling the pans.

4. Set out all your ingredients in a production line. Precut butter to tablespoon size; unload a five-pound bag of flour into a big bowl, and grind the nuts. You can also precut parchment paper to baking-pan size.

5. Try to make each type of cookie the same size, for easier stacking.

6. Once you're done baking, make sure any frosting or decoration is dry before packing.

7. Keep the cookies in airtight containers until just before they go into their gift boxes.

Flea markets and vintage-clothing stores are good sources for antique notions, like the golden knots used to border this cuff, made with a band of lush satin ribbon sewn directly on top of one of velvet. A length of satin or metallic ribbon serves as a hook.

STOCKINGS

An ordinary article of clothing serves as one of the season's most endearing signposts

There is something indescribably warm and pleasing about reaching

a hand into the snugness of a stocking and pulling out the tiny treasures

within. We like the size of the stocking, the compactness. A world

that can fit comfortably into a sock is a safe place, a child's dream.

A stocking pegged to a mantelpiece is perhaps the most personal item

of the holiday. Each member of the family has his own, a small sack

ranked in a row. It may be stitched from felt or old blanket wool,

or sewn from silk or satin or even see-through organza. However it

is put together, the **Christmas stocking** should

be as enticing and mysterious as any of the boxes beneath the tree.

STOCKING TEMPLATES

To make stockings and cuffs, simply enlarge these outlines on a copy machine (150 to 200 percent will make a typical stocking). Make sure that stockings and cuffs are enlarged in the same proportions. For the stocking, pin the patterns to two pieces of felt. Cut out the shapes, leaving a three-eighths-inch seam allowance. Pin the pieces together, wrong sides out, and sew all sides except top. Make small snips around the curves, being careful not to cut through the stitching (this will help the seams lie flat). Turn stocking right side out, smoothing side seams and the tip of the toe as you go along. Steam body and seam edges flat with an iron. To finish the top, turn it under about a half inch and press. At this point you can also attach a hanging loop.

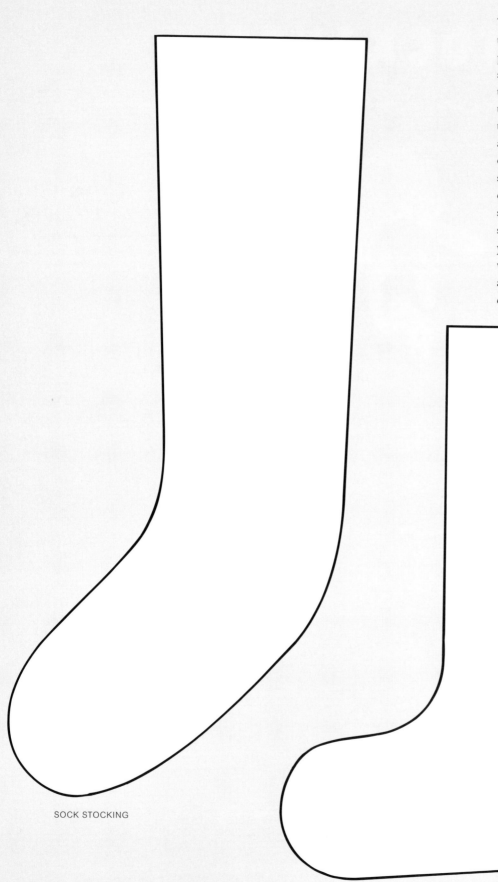

SOCK STOCKING

BOOT STOCKING

HIGH-HEEL STOCKING

TRADITIONAL STOCKING

45

CUFFS

THIS PAGE: Rich-hued blanket wools make cozy, traditional stockings. Use a different color to make a deep cuff (below) or toe and heel patches cut with straight or pinking shears (below right). Stitch the patches on by hand or attach with textile glue. The silver-bell-trimmed cuff is lined with a lightweight fabric; a wool lining can make the points too bulky. Design a name in stylized script, as on the socks at top right, inspired by the scrawls on cowboy shirts. Before sewing the stocking together, pin the name in ribbon or flat cotton cording to the fabric and hand-sew, using tiny stitches, with lightweight embroidery thread.

OPPOSITE: For a stocking that teases on Christmas morning with a seductive glimpse of its contents, use silk organza and cap it with taffeta. Organza, unlike velvet, is stiff enough to hold the shape of an upturned toe. To prevent the organza from fraying, enclose raw edges with a French seam or stitch up the sock inside out, then turn under and finish raw edges by hand.

FELT FLOWERS

Felt is a classic Christmas-stocking material. A combination of hat felts, available at millinery-supply houses, and standard, lighter-weight felt from the fabric store make for gorgeous textured blossoms. But standard felt works just fine on its own. The flowers can be sewn or glued onto the stocking. You may choose to cover an entire stocking with flowers, trim a cuff with them, or just use one or two blossoms as a bright accent.

RIGHT: Make daisies stand out on the stocking by using contrasting colors for the centers. For the tulip (also shown below), cut out a long, rounded rectangle of felt with one scalloped edge. Then fringe a smaller piece for the pistil. With the pistil inside, coil up the long piece of felt, stitching the base together by hand as you go.

BELOW RIGHT: For the star flower, you will need three pieces of felt. Place one piece on top of the other, arranging them so the petals overlap. Stitch together through middle of the flower, pulling so the pieces gather slightly. To make a layered flower, cut out leaf and petal shapes in various colors. Stack them, with a drop of textile glue between each layer, starting with leaves on the bottom. Stitch narrow strips on top to form the flower's pistil.

SMALL AND LARGE PETALS

These templates are shown at full size, but can be made larger or smaller by using a copy machine. If you plan to make a lot of flowers, consider tracing the shapes onto cardboard, which will last longer than paper templates.

POSY

TULIP

STAR FLOWER

LEAF

DAISY

PISTIL

A New York milliner inspired this fanciful stocking, bursting with leaves and flowers of many different hues (see previous pages for templates and directions).

BUTTONS

LEFT: Cream-colored felt is spruced up with a forest of quirky evergreens. The trees are trimmed with vintage glass buttons sewn on with thread in a contrasting color and then tacked onto the stocking with a few stitches.

BELOW: Most households have at least one drawer full of mismatched buttons. Put them to good use as a cuff for a plain, bright felt stocking. Or select a bagful of complementary colors from the miscellaneous-button box at a flea market or fabric store. This stocking is decorated with a collection of Bakelite buttons from the 1930s and 1940s.

CHRISTMAS TREE: Cut out the basic tree shape with a pair of scissors; then use pinking shears to create the delicate scalloped effect.

ORNAMENTS

Like precious jewels, they sparkle and enchant, forging a link between Christmases past, present, and future

They wait out the year in darkness, wrapped in tissue

paper and newsprint, inside old shoe boxes, in the corners of unused closets and

up in unlit attics. They are like time capsules waiting to

be uncovered, crystal and glass pieces brought briefly to life and set on

center stage, before they go back to their boxes.

Christmas ornaments are like family heirlooms; handed

down from generation to generation, they are often fancier and more ornate

than anything else in the house. For a few weeks they twirl and twinkle and flash.

They bell and jingle. They breathe.

While the glass globes and gilded angels are always welcome standbys, we like

to change our **ornaments,** adding different themes and designs

each year, experimenting with found objects and fashioning new creations out of just about anything:

dried fruit, seed pods, walnuts, ribbons, seashells, or starfish.

We save the best of each year's crop, stashing them away with the old ornaments.

In this way, we create our own heirlooms for the future,

increasing the contents of our special time capsule.

OPPOSITE: On or off a tree, ornaments add dazzle. Stacked in a vase (left), these glass balls catch the sunlight. Sea urchins (right) are dressed up in gold and silver.

THIS PAGE: Martha Stewart used 260 moon- and star-shaped gingerbread cookies, along with vintage mercury-glass balls and wide satin ribbon, to decorate this Norway spruce.

FROM THE KITCHEN

baking ornaments

Though the same recipe may be used to make ornamental gingerbread cookies or a gingerbread house, not every recipe is suitable. Ours produces pieces that will hold their shape well, with smooth surfaces and sharp edges. The pieces won't shrink or warp, which is especially important when constructing a house. This recipe can easily be doubled, but shouldn't be increased any further.

To make the house, cut out individual pieces from the dough before baking, or roll out one large piece the size of a cookie sheet, bake it, and cut out the house parts as soon as it comes out of the oven.

If you use silver dragées, remember that they are for decoration only and not to be consumed. The cookies and house will last the entire season, but should not be kept for the next year.

LEFT AND ABOVE: Martha's moons and stars are strung on fine silver cord that she found at a fabric store.

BELOW LEFT AND RIGHT: To decorate cookies, spread a layer of icing on each and decorate with silver dragées in assorted sizes.

OPPOSITE, ABOVE: Place finished decorated cookies on a parchment-lined baking sheet and allow icing to dry before hanging on a tree.

OPPOSITE, BELOW: For additional house decoration, we made a wood pile out of cinnamon sticks (held together with a bit of icing), and arranged pine needles around the house. Confectioners' sugar was sifted over everything to simulate freshly fallen snow.

gingerbread ornaments and house

makes enough for twelve 6-inch
ornaments or 1 house

6 cups all-purpose flour
1 teaspoon baking soda
½ teaspoon baking powder
½ pound (2 sticks) unsalted butter
1 cup dark brown sugar
4 teaspoons ground ginger
4 teaspoons ground cinnamon
1½ teaspoons ground cloves
1 teaspoon finely ground pepper
1½ teaspoons salt
2 large eggs
1½ cups unsulfured molasses
Royal Icing Glaze and Stiff Royal
Icing (recipes follow)

1. In a large bowl, sift together flour,
baking soda, and baking powder. Set aside.
2. In the bowl of an electric mixer fitted
with the paddle attachment, cream butter
and brown sugar until fluffy. Mix in
spices and salt. Beat in eggs and molasses.
3. Add the flour mixture and mix on low
speed until thoroughly combined. Divide
dough into thirds and wrap in plastic.
Chill at least 1 hour.
4. Heat oven to 350°. On a well-floured
surface, roll out dough to ⅛ inch. Cut into
desired shapes. Place on an ungreased baking
sheet and chill until firm, about 15 minutes.
Bake 12 to 15 minutes for cookies, 15 minutes or more for house pieces. The gingerbread should be firm in the center but not
darker around the edges.
5. When cookies are just out of the oven,
use a skewer to make a small hole ½ inch
from top of each one to accommodate a
hook or cord. Cool completely on wire racks
before decorating with Royal Icing Glaze.
6. Let house pieces cool, then assemble with
Stiff Royal Icing. Spoon into a pastry bag
fitted with a No. 5 plain tip. Pipe a line
along edges of sides, back, and front. Attach
roof pieces and place on house. Assemble

chimney pieces and attach to the roof.
7. For decorating, thin icing slightly with
water but don't allow to become too liquid.
Pipe to outline windows, doorway, chimney,
and 4 joining points of house. Outline roof;
pipe a scallop pattern over its surface.

royal icing glaze
makes about 2 cups

2 large egg whites (see Note, below)
4 cups (1 pound) sifted confectioners' sugar
Juice of 1 lemon
3 drops glycerine (available at
pharmacies)

Beat the egg whites until stiff but not dry.
Add sugar, lemon juice, and glycerine and
beat for 1 minute more. Icing should be
spreadable; if it's too thick, add more lemon
juice; if too thin, add more sugar.

NOTE: Raw eggs should not be used in
food prepared for pregnant women, babies,
young children, or anyone whose health
is compromised.

stiff royal icing
makes 3 cups

3 large egg whites (see Note, above)
5 cups (1¼ pounds) sifted confectioners' sugar

In the bowl of an electric mixer, beat egg
whites on low speed until just frothy, 1
minute. Beat in ¼ cup sugar. Add remaining
sugar and beat icing on high speed until it
holds a peak and is very thick, 5 to 10 minutes. To keep a crust from forming, cover icing with a damp paper towel.

GINGERBREAD HOUSE TEMPLATES

The template below is full size, but you can use a copy machine to enlarge or reduce it as you wish. You can also use this design as a starting point for creating your own house. Trace the pieces on parchment paper (or cardboard, for a sturdier template) and cut out. Now cut the dough into appropriate shapes, making sure to cut duplicate pieces where required (omit the door for the back). For the cleanest edges, use a very sharp knife.

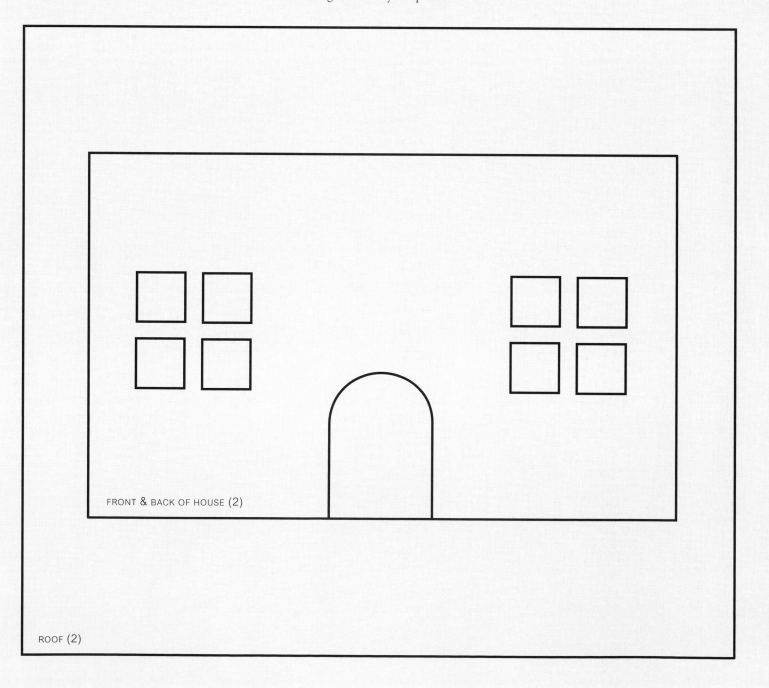

FRONT & BACK OF HOUSE (2)

ROOF (2)

FRONT & BACK OF CHIMNEY (1 EACH)

SIDES OF CHIMNEY (1 EACH)

SIDES OF HOUSE (2)

FRUIT & MILLINERY ORNAMENTS

Millinery notions, lightweight dried fruit, and ribbon (opposite) become arboreal jewelry with very little effort. In addition to fruit, you can try working with painted or gilded nuts, rattlebox beans, milkweed, or seed pods.

BELOW: Dried oranges are wrapped in contrasting colors of sheer organdy, two and three inches wide. Gather two twelve-inch-long pieces around fruit and tie together with satin ribbon, which can then be used as a loop for hanging. For best results, use commercially freeze-dried fruit: Drying fruit at home can take several months and yield uneven results (see The Guide for sources).

OPPOSITE: Clusters of millinery fruit in sun-drenched colors are tied with bows of sheer organdy ribbon. Hooks can be attached to the ribbon for hanging.

THIS PAGE: These lush-looking grapes are tied directly to the tree with ribbon.

RIBBON STAR

This delicate star ornament is a traditional German holiday decoration originally made from strips of paper. To keep these fragile ornaments from being crushed between holidays, wrap them in tissue and store side by side in a flat box.

1. Start with a 72" length of ⅝"-wide ribbon. We used a vintage metallic weave, but any stiff, double-faced, heavyweight cloth or paper ribbon would also work well. Cut ribbon into four 18" lengths, trimming ends into points. (If using cloth ribbon, wrap tips with masking tape). Fold each length in half. On a flat surface, lay two folded ribbons vertically, one with tips facing up, the other down. Take a third folded ribbon and weave through paired ribbons, working from right to left: Pass through right-hand ribbon so that bottom length goes through center, top length over top; pass through left-hand ribbon so that both lengths go through center. Take fourth folded ribbon and weave through paired ribbons in the same way, working from left to right. Arrange ribbons as shown so that a square is created at center.

2. Pull tips away from center to form an interlaced knot.

3. Take upper piece of ribbon emerging to the right and fold it to the left, over knot. Do the same with upper piece of ribbon emerging to the left, folding it to the right.

4. Take upper piece of ribbon emerging at the top and weave it toward bottom: Pass over top ribbon fold and through loop under bottom fold. Pull tight. Repeat with upper piece of the ribbon emerging at bottom. You will now have a center knot with eight emerging ribbons of two different lengths heading in each direction.

5. Fold the lower of the two right-pointing ribbons down and under itself at a 90° angle; crease. Then circle it up over triangle you've created and tuck tip though adjacent loop, as shown. Pull tight to create the first star point.

6. Rotate knot counterclockwise a quarter turn. Repeat step 5. Rotate and repeat twice more.

7. Rotate one last turn and flip knot over.

8. Lift the upper of the two top-pointing tips, exposing loop underneath. Weave through loop; pull tight. Repeat with the upper of the two bottom-pointing tips.

9. Create four more star points as in step 5, using upper ribbons. You will now have eight emerging ribbons, four of them under points, four over.

10. To make outward-pointing star points: Lift the top right-pointing ribbon. Fold it upward under itself at a 90° angle and crease. Curve ribbon to left and down under adjacent piece of top-pointing ribbon; thread tip through loop (tip will emerge through center of point). Pull taut. Rotate knot counterclockwise and repeat, threading through loop under new projecting point. Repeat twice more. Make one more quarter turn and flip star over. Repeat folding process on the other side with four remaining ribbon ends. When finished, trim ribbon ends flush with the points from which they emerge. Dot both sides of ends inside points with craft glue and press points together to secure. Hang star from the tree by a hook or a loop of thread.

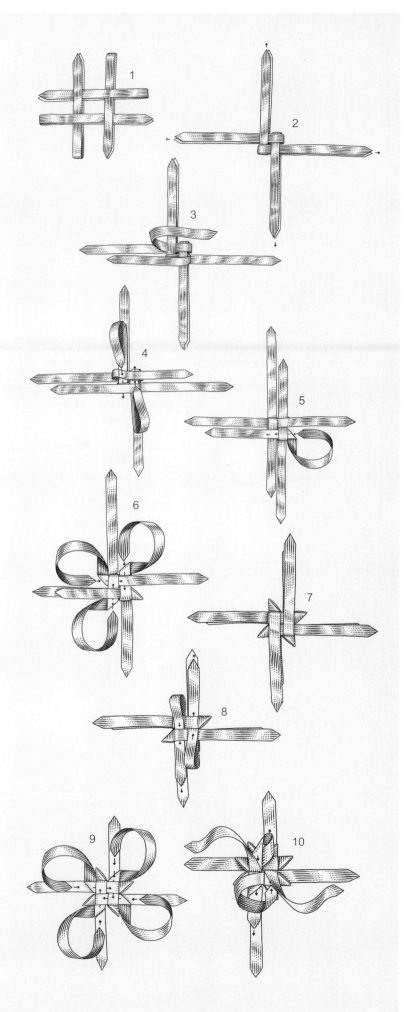

VINTAGE ORNAMENTS

Most of us have a box that holds cherished old ornaments. Heirlooms eagerly brought forth from storage each year—as well as decades-old pieces picked up at antiques shops—aren't just tree trimmings: They're cultural artifacts and talismans.

The Germans started the custom of decorating Christmas trees in the seventeenth century, hanging cookies, candies, paper flowers and fruits. By the nineteenth century, they had progressed to glass globes, called Kugels ("hollow balls"). Today, a lovely but plain round Kugel in a common color like silver might be found for a few dollars at a flea market, while a rarer shape in colors like red or amethyst might go for $1000 or more. Also ripe for collecting is the Dresden, an elaborately detailed silvered and gilded cardboard ornament named for the town where it was first manufactured.

Adornments of a more recent vintage can be relatively inexpensive and are especially appropriate for homes with small children. Ornaments from the 1960s—for instance, something painted with a psychedelic daisy—can still be found at tag sales. In addition to being affordable, these post–World War II decorations have a certain kitschy charm. And while a skiing plastic-and-pipe-cleaner Santa, say, may not be as refined as a Victorian glass bird, it evokes its own sort of memories.

If you treat your vintage ornaments with care, your children and grandchildren will be able to get as much enjoyment from them as you did. Never wash antique ornaments, since many were painted with water-based colors; dusting with a soft brush is sufficient. To store, wrap them in acid-free tissue paper (some dealers tuck them inside an air-filled Ziploc bag, which provides a cushion against breakage) and store in a compartmentalized box. Moisture-trapping packs of silica gel (available at floral-supply and craft stores) inside the packing will also help preserve painted surfaces and prevent mildew. Finally, avoid putting the ornaments away in attics and basements, which are prone to fluctuations in temperature and humidity.

ornament tree

It doesn't take long for ornament collectors to acquire enough glass balls to decorate a miniature tree. With age, these balls take on the soft patina of worn metal. To make a glass tree, you'll need an 18"-high Styrofoam cone and approximately 250 balls ranging in size from ½" to 1" in diameter. Starting at the bottom of the cone, hot glue balls one at a time, starting with the largest (left). Hold in place until the glue dries, about 1 minute. An antique garden urn (below) is the perfect pot for this golden tree.

GIFTS FROM THE SEA

Until F. W. Woolworth and his five-and-dime stores brought glass balls to the masses, families made Christmas-tree decorations from found objects, which represented the recurring motifs in their lives. Queen Victoria and Prince Albert loved sweets; their tree was decorated with bonbons and gingerbread. Berliners gilded potatoes and beets; Austrians used apples and nuts. Pioneer families in America hung ears of corn, dried seed pods, and honey cakes. Mississippians, who don't live in evergreen country, decorated sassafrass trees with hickory nuts and hawthorn fruit. Swedish immigrants in the early 1900s hung their trees with silver knives, forks and spoons.

Seashells also make personal, idiosyncratic decorations. In bleak midwinter, they hold the taste of last summer's sea air and the memory of scavenging for these treasures in the sand. Gilded, silvered, twined with ribbons, dotted with shimmering balls, the shells are transformed. The otherworldly ornaments on these pages were made with the most prosaic equipment: a hot-glue gun; an electric drill with a one-sixteenth-inch bit for making holes in brittle shell; ribbon; thread; and a collection of silver and gold dragées.

LEFT: Silver dragées have been hot-glued to a trochus shell; a pendant clasp from a jewelry-findings supplier holds the thread to hang the delicate ornament.

FAR LEFT: A Pacific starfish is outlined with gold cord attached with a hot-glue gun; a pearl-headed hat pin is pushed through the top of an arm to hold gilt thread.

NEAR LEFT: Using similar methods, ordinary glass ornaments can be turned into intriguing adornments. Here, dragées of different sizes have been hot-glued to the glass, and silver cord wrapped around the top.

ABOVE RIGHT: Pearl-tipped hat pins decorate a starfish. Snip off the metal pin with pliers, then dab a bit of glue on the pearl to secure it to the shell. To hang, make two holes at the top of one of the arms and tie a length of silver cord through the holes.

ABOVE FAR RIGHT: Sea urchins, studded with dragées and wound with gold twine, look like Renaissance jewels. The techniques used to turn these shells into ornaments could transform almost any found object: leaves and seed pods can be dried, painted, and tied with gold ribbon; nuts and eggshells can be gilded or silvered and then decorated with dragées.

RIGHT: A starfish resting in the shell of a giant clam is bound with gold gauze ribbon frayed to resemble tinsel. A dragée is glued to the center, and gilt thread is tied through a tiny hole drilled at the end of an arm.

BELOW: Gold and silver braid follow the curves of auger shells; pearl-headed hat pins are pushed through the centers and fixed with glue.

67

OPPOSITE: Strands of tiny white lights strung through the trees make the seashell ornaments glow. Each tree is crowned with a giant starfish.

THIS PAGE: A dragée-studded sand star is draped across nineteenth-century German ornaments—hollow blown-glass spheres with mercury swirled inside.

WIRING

ribbon garland

OPPOSITE: Stylist David McLean tops this white spruce with a papier-mâché finch. More than three hundred artificial fruits and birds, found at the San Francisco flower market, decorate the tree. Each ornament came with wire attached, so binding them to the branches was easy. McLean encircled his bright and animated tree with colored lights and a billowing red garland. At the top of the tree, he tied the ribbon in a big bow. To make the garland (above right), sandwich florist's wire between two velveteen ribbons, and secure with rubber cement, spreading the glue out to the edges of the ribbon. Use push pins to hold the wire in place and keep the ribbons taut as you glue.

ORNAMENT WIRE

For secure attachment, thread fine-grade wire or green florist's wire through the loop on the ornament and twist the ends to secure it.

pinecone garland

As autumn turns to winter, the yard is blanketed with fallen pinecones. Rather than sweep them into the trash or compost, gather the cones for a holiday garland that can decorate a doorway or tree. Use an awl, a nail, or a drill with a small bit (a three-thirty-second- or one-eighth-inch bit will do) to puncture holes at the base of the cones. Next, using a heavy-weight darning needle, string the cones together with carpet thread or fine floral wire (available at most florists). For a festive touch, intersperse the cones with silver Victorian beads or jewelry beads of almost any size.

EARTHLY DELIGHTS

Jerry Bolduan, a doctor who left his private practice to grow flowers in Sebastopol, California, has been making Christmas decorations since he was twelve. For the Colorado blue spruce, opposite, he designed more than a dozen different kinds of natural ornaments. Before hanging even one, he interlaced the branches with two thousand tiny white lights. "The ornaments aren't shiny, so lots of lights are needed," Bolduan says. He recommends hanging the lights one day, ornaments the next.

LEFT: Bolduan hot-glued nigella pods, hemlock and spruce cones, freeze-dried rosebuds, poppy pods, cockscomb, and bleached Siberian-iris pods to papier-mâché balls from a variety store. The maple wings were sprayed with water-based urethane and sprinkled with mica granules (available at crafts stores).

BELOW: Bolduan used a small Dremel Moto-Tool drill to make holes in acorns and hemlock cones before stringing them on fishing line, with alternating tiny gold and silver beads. He used a needle and cotton thread to string rosebud garlands.

These pinecones were sprayed with silver and gold paint. Metallic cord was attached with pearl-headed hat pins.

"I wanted to use natural colors to make a rich brocade," says Jerry Bolduan of his extravagantly decorated tree.

GIFTS

Presents you make yourself are sure ways to express your love

Gift-giving is a ritual at least as old as the Magi. But while the three wise men

carried precious substances to Bethlehem, the expense of their gifts was less important than their

intention and presentation, a principle every gift giver should consider. A gift from the heart,

presented with grace, can be the most precious of all. In this chapter, we'll show you how to

personalize any gift by placing it in a box you have built or found and enhanced

with ribbons, tassels, or silk. We will also suggest ways to make unusual gifts

from ordinary materials. Even more special are products you make yourself.

Our suggestions include homemade pickles, candies, and breads as well

as sachets and potpourris that will fill the recipient's home with scents for months to come.

Not frankincense or myrrh, perhaps, but every bit as special.

Most gifts come in boxes that are obsolete once they've been opened. A pyramid box, made from chipboard and finished with gold paper and cord, is a worthy gift in and of itself.

KEEPSAKE BOXES

pyramid box

1. Using a compass, draw a circle with a 2" radius on single-weight chipboard. From the center, mark five 72° segments on the perimeter with a protractor. Connect the marks to form a pentagon. Open compass the length of one side, place its point at *b*, and draw an arc. From *c* draw an arc intersecting the first to make point *d*. Extend a straight line from the center *a* through *d* to a point *e* 9" from *a*. Repeat for all five sides. Complete triangles to form a star. With an X-Acto knife and straightedge, cut out pentagon and triangles separately.

2. Split the chipboard at tip of each triangle and glue in narrow 12" ribbons.

3. Cut five 2½"-by-1" lengths of kraft paper, trimming off corners. Spread glue on one side of each piece, and use like tape to bond triangles to pentagon. Dry flat. Place star, tape side up, on a 20"-by-20" sheet of colored paper and trace around it, with a ½" allowance on

all sides but tapering inward at points. Cut out tracing. Spread glue on underside of pentagon; attach paper. Glue triangles separately, holding at a right angle to base. Fold in allowance; glue flat.

4. Cut a slightly smaller star from contrasting paper and glue to inside of box. To close box, thread ribbons through a bead. The finished product, opposite, is an irresistible temptation.

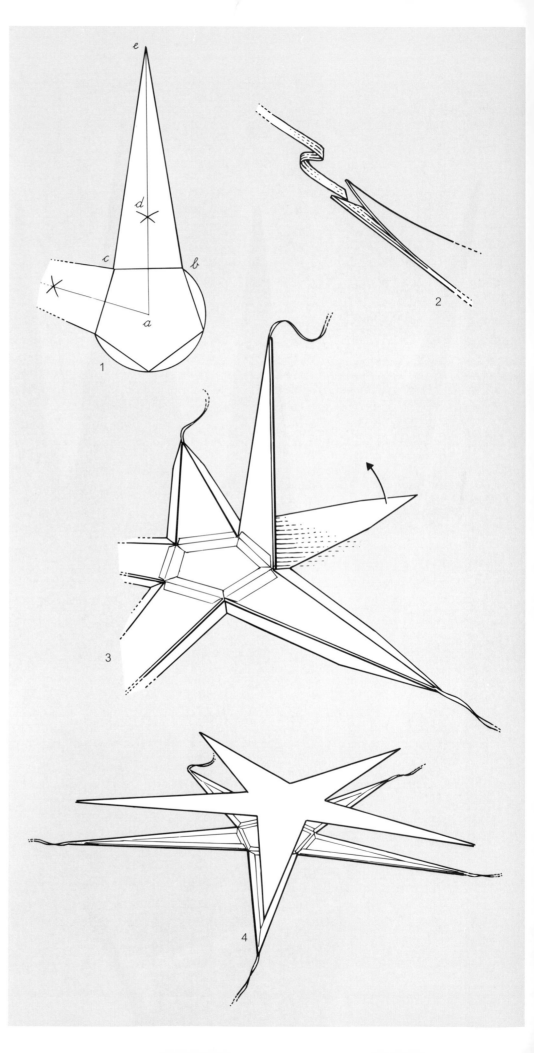

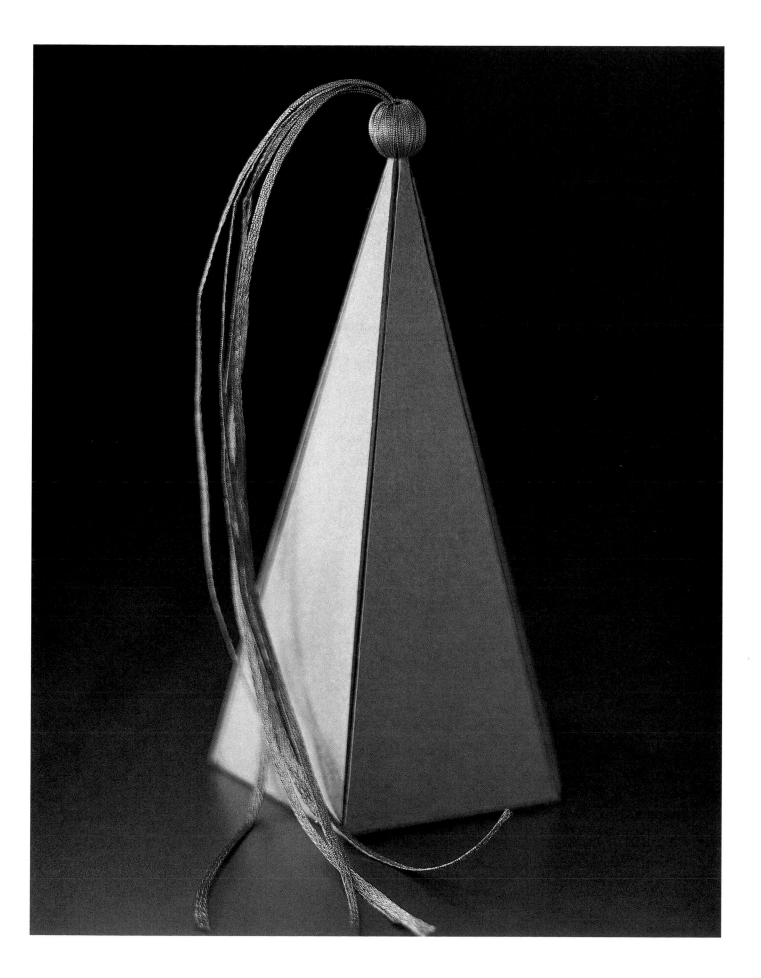

A cardboard mailing tube is the basis for an elegant tasseled box (see page 80 for instructions on how to make).

An ordinary cardboard cigar box becomes a refined receptacle when it's covered in silk and stuffed with cotton batting. A decorative button serves as a closure.

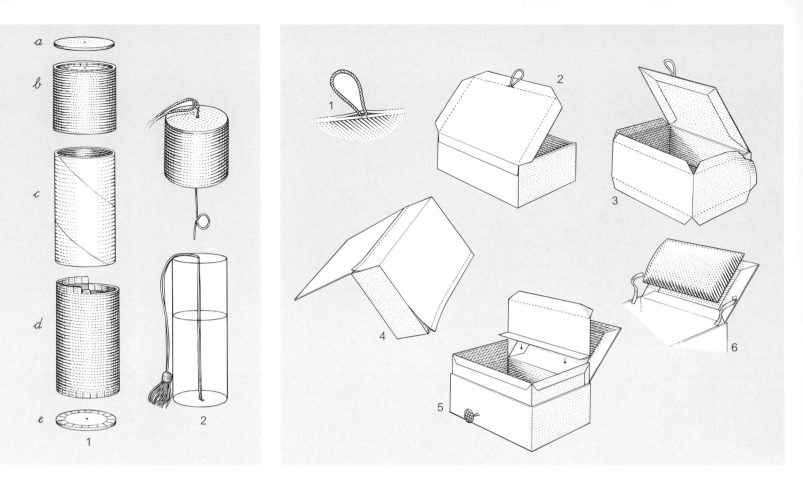

tasseled box

1. Remove the inner tube (*c*) from a postal cylinder and cut off a section 1" longer than cylinder's lid (which will become the bottom of the box). Set aside. To make the box lid (*b*), shorten bottom of cylinder to a height of 3". Cover outside of the top and bottom (*d*) parts of box with silk, enough to overlap 1" where the fabric meets and with a ½" allowance at each end. At the seam, turn the fabric under and glue flat. At each end of both parts of box, snip into allowance all around and glue down one section at a time. Poke a hole in the center of each metal end piece. Cut two cardboard circles (*a* and *e*) to fit end pieces and cover the pieces with silk. Poke a hole through the center of the top circle. Glue this circle to the box top. Glue the inner tube into the bottom of the box.

2. Thread a cord through the hole in the bottom of the box, allowing its length to be one and a half times the height of box. Secure the cord to the underside with tape. Pass it through hole in the top, and attach a tassel to the end. Glue the second cardboard circle (*e*) to bottom of box.

silk cigar box

1. Split open front edge of cardboard cigar box lid; glue a loop of elasticized cord inside.

2. Cut a piece of silk to fit lid, with a ½" allowance on all sides. Glue fabric to the outside of lid. Cut a slit in the fabric at front edge and pull loop through. Trim corners and glue allowance to inside of lid and back of box.

3. Cut a piece of silk to cover front and sides, with a ½" allowance. Glue silk to one side at a time. Trim corners; glue allowance over edges.

4. Cover the back and bottom of box with a panel of silk whose ½" allowance has been turned under and glued flat.

5. Poke a hole through the center front of box and secure a button from the inside. To make ribbon hinges for the lid, cut two 1"-wide strips of fabric. Turn long edges under, fold in half lengthwise, and glue flat. Glue into place. Line inside walls of box with silk, turning under and gluing the allowance flat along top edges.

6. To pad interior, cut two cardboard panels just smaller than lid. Using cotton batting, form a plump pillow for the bottom of box and a thinner one for lid; attach batting to panels. Cover with silk; glue pillows into box.

acorn box

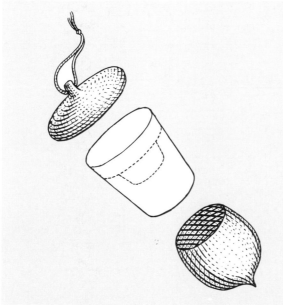

Gently remove the cap from a newly fallen acorn. Carve out the white circle underneath and remove the soft meat from inside the acorn. Wrap fine-grade sandpaper around a pencil eraser and smooth the inside of the acorn shell. Stain the outside with wood stain and allow to dry overnight. Select a cork that fits snugly into the acorn cap. Shorten the cork and carve to fit into the acorn opening. Smooth the cork with sandpaper and glue into cap. Drill a hole through the acorn's stem, and attach a loop of ribbon.

FRAMES

copper-tape frame

Anything looks better in a frame, and a simple structure fashioned from copper-foil tape and glass or Plexiglas makes a lovely gift. Ferns, leaves, and flowers can be sandwiched between sheets of glass for a see-through effect, but works on paper like the engraving, above right, should be matted and topped with glazing to keep them from sticking in humid weather.

Start with two sheets of thin glass or Plexiglas (or one sheet and a matted image). Frames that are bigger than a picture book should use Plexiglas, which is lighter than glass and won't shatter.

After positioning the object or mat under glazing, tape edges together along two parallel sides with half-inch-wide self-stick copper-foil tape, leaving a quarter inch extra at each end (left). Be sure tape edges are even along the frame front. Snip tape ends in along corner folds to meet glazing, then fold the pieces neatly over one another.

Smooth tape against glazing with a fingernail. Tape the remaining two sides, trimming ends flush to glazing. If you prefer a dark finish, like ours, to shiny copper, lightly roughen the tape using fine-grade steel wool, and paint on a tarnishing agent such as Jax Brass, Bronze & Copper Darkener (below left).

shell mirror

Collecting shells for a homemade mirror (right) gives beachcombing a purpose. Scrub and soak shells in soap and water, or lighten in a solution of bleach and water; dry thoroughly. Paint the front of a flat wooden picture frame white or pastel. Use black paint for the underside and inside edge, which will be reflected in the mirror. Mercury mirror glass, available at fine glass stores, is well suited to weathered shells. Have the glass cut to size; a framing store can secure it to the back of the wood. Sort your shells by size, shape, and color; arrange on the frame in even rows, using delicate shells to line the inner edge (below, far right), full shells for the middle row, and flat scallops or cockles to form a fluted border. Glue down one at a time using extra-thick craft glue.

pinecone frame

An engraved bookplate rests inside a pinecone frame (below). Apply a dark wood stain to frame, then hot-glue same-size pinecones to front in two outward-facing rows (below right). Nestle a third row on top; glue in place.

velvet scarves

Velvet is one of the most luxurious of fabrics. Antique velvet, often found as dress remnants, is especially smooth to the touch; scarves are a good use for these one-of-a-kind finds.

To make the green antique-velvet scarf, cut a remnant 1½ yards long and at least ½ yard wide. Cut a piece of silk charmeuse the same size for backing. With right sides facing, align fabrics and machine-stitch a ½" seam around edges, leaving 12" open on one long side. Clip corners on a diagonal and turn right side out. Hand-stitch the opening.

To make the brown new-velvet scarf, cut two pieces of velvet 2 yards long and 16" wide and sew together as described above. Then machine-stitch ¼" from edges to keep the velvet from rolling.

SMALL LUXURIES

ribbon tray

This ribbon tray can be assembled easily in under an hour. You'll need a flat-bottomed tray, either square or rectangular; a sheet of glass and a piece of corrugated cardboard, both cut to fit inside the tray; masking tape; and satin ribbon. We used one-inch-wide ribbon in five colors, about three yards of each.

1. Alternating two colors, stretch ribbon strips tautly across the cardboard; tape ends to underside.

2. Working lengthwise, weave a third color ribbon over and under attached strips, pulling woven strip firmly to one side of cardboard before taping to back. Repeat with a fourth color, pulling ribbon tightly against previous one before securing. Repeat with fifth color; continue until cardboard is covered. For a varied effect, use ribbons of different widths.

3. Slide woven cardboard onto tray bottom and cover with clean quarter-inch-thick glass (four times the thickness of a windowpane). Although this will add substantial weight to the tray, glass any thinner may crack under a heavy load of china or glassware. If your tray is large, consider using Plexiglas, which scratches more easily but is much lighter.

little fabric books

A blank book is such a personal possession that it deserves a personalized cover. Any fabric can be pressed into service: Just use dark fabric if the original cover is black.

1. Open the book flat and cut fabric to fit, adding 2" to all sides. Using a stencil brush, apply fabric glue to front cover. Let dry for 30 seconds. Lay fabric over the glue, lining the pattern up with the book's edges. With a bone folder (a bookbinding tool available at art-supply stores), press fabric into glue. Use the tip to push the fabric into the gutter alongside the spine.

2. Apply glue to the spine and back cover of book. Pull fabric around into the second gutter using the bone folder, then smooth it onto the back of the book.

3. Open the front cover. Notch fabric at each corner as shown, leaving ⅛" of fabric at the point of the V to wrap over the corner. Apply glue to edges of inside cover, wrap corners, then fold remaining fabric inside and smooth it onto the glue. Repeat for back-cover edges. At top and bottom of the spine, cut fabric down to ¼" from the book's edge. Turn to the inside and glue flat. To line inside covers, cut two fabric panels ¾" larger than covers on all sides. Fold a 1" hem all around and iron flat. Apply glue to inside covers of book and attach panels. If you like, an identification label can be glued to front of book.

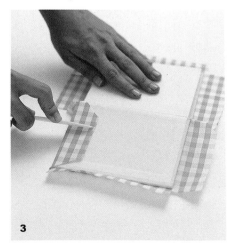

silver holders

Cases made from tarnish-resistant cloth protect silver so it doesn't have to be polished with each use. The fabric, soft cotton flannel treated with zinc, is sold by the yard at fabric stores. The pocketed flatware roll, left, is made from two pieces, one 12" by 13½" and the other 10" by 10". Sew a ¼" hem on one side of smaller piece; this will be the top edge of the pocket. Align bottom right corners of both pieces and hem remaining edges. Topstitch parallel seams to make pockets, each ½" wider and ½" shorter than the piece of flatware it will hold. To tie, hand-stitch an 18" piece of ribbon to outside of roll, 3" from left edge.

fabric-wrapped packages

Sometimes, appearances are everything. A container draped in luxurious cloth is a sophisticated gift regardless of what's inside. To make one of the packages above, choose two squares of raw material, such as silk and satin. Place the right sides of the cloth facing each other and sew the edges together, leaving a two-inch gap at one end. Turn the whole thing inside out and hand-stitch the opening. Position gift diagonally across the center of the square and wrap two opposing corners tightly around the item. Tie the remaining pair into a knot and tuck in any loose edges. A pair of knots makes the package look more playful.

PICKLED
FENNEL
'94

Pickled fennel, flanked here by fresh fennel and whole oranges, is ready to eat the day after it is prepared. Label each jar with the pickle's name and date of preparation.

pickled fennel
makes 3 pints

Serve this quick pickle between courses to cleanse the palate.

- 3 pounds fennel (about 9 bulbs)
- 1 medium orange
- 2 cups white vinegar
- 5 tablespoons kosher salt
- 2 tablespoons sugar
- 6 whole pieces star anise

1. Wash 3 pint jars and lids in hot soapy water and rinse well. (You can use canning jars and lids, but you don't have to.)
2. Wash fennel and cut away any bruises or bad spots. Trim the ends and slice into very thin rings. Cut three 1-inch-long strips of peel from the orange; remove any pith.
3. Bring 1½ cups water, the vinegar, salt, and sugar to a boil in a large pot.
4. Meanwhile, fill each jar halfway with fennel. Place 1 piece of orange rind and 2 pieces star anise on top of fennel. Fill jar with remaining fennel, using the back of a clean spoon to pack it down. Leave ¾ inch of space beneath the rim.
5. Pour hot liquid over fennel, covering it by ¼ inch and leaving ½ inch of space beneath the rim of each jar. Place lids on jars and let stand until cool. Store in refrigerator; serve within 5 days.

pickled okra
makes 6 pints

These dill pickles are a worthy rival to the standard cucumber pickle.

- 2 pounds tender okra
- 1 quart white vinegar
- 6 tablespoons kosher salt
- 16 small cloves garlic, peeled
- 8 small fresh hot red peppers, such as New Mexican chile or Mirasol
- 1 bunch fresh dill (about 24 sprigs)
- ½ cup yellow mustard seeds

1. Rinse okra; cut away any bruises or bad spots. Trim stem ends of okra but do not remove caps entirely.
2. Wash 8 one-pint canning jars, lids, and screw bands with hot, soapy water and rinse well. Place jars upright on a wire rack in the bottom of a large pot. Fill pot with hot water until jars are submerged by 1 to 2 inches; bring to a boil. Boil for 15 minutes. Turn off heat, leaving jars in water. Sterilize lids according to manufacturer's instructions.
3. Meanwhile, bring vinegar, 3 cups water, and salt to a boil in a large pot.
4. Using stainless-steel tongs, remove jars from water; set on a layer of clean towels. Evenly divide garlic, peppers, dill sprigs, and mustard seeds among jars. Pack tightly with okra, alternating direction of caps. Leave ¾ inch of space beneath rim of jar. Pour hot liquid over okra, covering it by ¼ inch and leaving ½ inch of space beneath rim. Slide a clean wooden skewer along inside of each jar to release air bubbles. Wipe mouth of jar with a clean, damp cloth. Place hot lid on jar; turn screw band firmly without forcing.
5. Place a wire rack in the bottom of a large pot and fill partway with hot water. Using a jar lifter, place jars on rack. Add hot water to cover by 2 inches, and bring to a boil. Boil for 10 minutes. Remove jars from water bath; let stand on clean dish towels for 24 hours. Check cool jars for the slight indentation in lids that indicates a vacuum seal. Jars that do not seal properly or that leak during processing should be refrigerated and consumed within a week. Allow sealed pickles to mellow in a cool, dry place for 6 to 8 weeks before serving. Store opened jars in refrigerator.

BELOW: Pickling gear (left) includes jars, lids screwbands, a wide-mouthed funnel and tongs. Jars with chips or cracks should be discarded. Martha Stewart and Salli LaGrone (right) use ladles to spoon the pickles into clean, sterilized jars.

brandied pears
makes about 3 quarts

The pears need about a month to absorb the brandy. Make a few jars before Thanksgiving to give for Christmas.

- ¼ cup fresh lemon juice (about 2 lemons)
- 5½ pounds Seckel pears (about 20)
- 1½ cups sugar
- 2 cinnamon sticks
- 3 cups brandy

1. Fill a large bowl half full of cold water and add lemon juice. Peel pears as carefully and smoothly as possible, leaving stems attached. Place pears in water as you peel them.
2. Combine sugar, cinnamon sticks, and 3 quarts water in a large stockpot. Drain pears and add to pot. Bring mixture to a boil, reduce heat, and simmer for 10 to 30 minutes, depending on size and ripeness of pears.
3. Remove pears from liquid with a slotted spoon and divide evenly among 3 quart jars.
4. Raise heat under pot to high and cook liquid until reduced to 2 cups, about 50 minutes. Remove from heat; strain liquid into a bowl through a sieve lined with cheesecloth. Divide the liquid evenly among the jars and add about 1 cup of brandy, or enough to cover pears, to each. Allow jars to cool and screw on lids. Refrigerate for several weeks before eating to allow flavors to develop.

ABOVE: A jar of brandied pears can be dressed up with a round of colored paper, gold rope or twine, and a wax seal.

⅓ cup warm water
2 packages (2½ teaspoons each)
  active dry yeast
4 cups all-purpose flour
½ cup warm milk
⅔ cup sugar
4 large eggs
2 large egg yolks
1 teaspoon vanilla extract
12 tablespoons (1½ sticks)
  unsalted butter
2 cups mixed dried and candied fruit
  Zest of 1 lemon
  Zest of 1 orange
3 3⅜-by-7½-inch brown paper bags
2 tablespoons melted butter, for bags
1 large egg yolk mixed with 1
  tablespoon heavy cream, for
  egg wash

1. To make the sponge, warm a small bowl by rinsing it with hot water. Pour in warm water and sprinkle 1 package yeast on it. Let stand until yeast has dissolved. Stir in ½ cup flour, cover with plastic wrap, and let stand for 30 minutes, or until doubled.
2. Sprinkle remaining yeast over warm milk. Let stand until dissolved.
3. Beat together sugar, eggs, egg yolks, and vanilla. Mix in yeast-milk mixture. Add sponge and stir until well incorporated.
4. Combine butter and remaining 3½ cups flour until crumbly. Slowly pour in egg mixture and beat on high speed for 3 to 4 minutes, until dough is elastic-looking and long strands form. Beat in fruit and zests. Turn dough into an oiled bowl, cover with plastic wrap, and leave in a warm place to rise until doubled, 2 to 3 hours.
5. Fold down bags to form a 3-inch cuff. Brush inside and out with melted butter.
6. Turn out dough onto a lightly floured board and knead a few times to deflate. Divide dough into 3 pieces. Roll each into a ball and drop into prepared bags. Place bags on a baking sheet about 4 inches apart and cover loosely with plastic wrap. Let rise in a warm place until doubled again, about 2 hours.
7. Heat oven to 400°. Cut an X in top of each loaf with oiled scissors. Brush tops lightly with egg wash. Place baking sheet in bottom third of oven. After 10 minutes, lower heat to 375°. Bake for 30 more minutes; if tops get too brown, cover with foil. Loaves are done when a wooden skewer inserted into centers comes out clean. Cool on a wire rack.

Two European creations make delectable gifts for the holidays. The French term for button candies is *nonpareils,* which means "without peer." No one who remembers these candies from childhood would argue with that appellation. Dark chocolate buttons topped with sugar beads, nonpareils (above and below) are the caviar of childhood.

Panettone (opposite) is the traditional Italian Christmas bread originally from Milan. Eggy and moist, with an irresistible aroma, it's an appealing alternative to the venerable—and overfamiliar—fruitcake. Bake it in small portions (the Italian versions are usually heftier) in buttered brown-paper bags.

nonpareils
makes about 50

8 ounces bittersweet chocolate
½ teaspoon vegetable shortening
¼ cup sugar beads

Line a baking sheet with parchment paper; set aside. Melt together chocolate and shortening in the top of a double boiler. Spoon chocolate in nickel-size circles onto baking sheet. Cool for 20 minutes; sprinkle with sugar beads. Let nonpareils harden for 4 hours before packing into a box.

These small golden loaves of panettone were
baked in buttered paper bags, then tied up
with string.

SCENTED GIFTS

flavored sugars

A mason jar filled with scented sugar, right, is a simple but inventive gift. Layer granulated sugar with aromatic, edible items like rose petals, scented-geranium leaves, orange and lemon peel (first set out for a day to dry), or vanilla beans. The result is an exotic sweetener that adds a subtle perfume and flavor to coffee, fruit desserts, and baked goods. Mix up small batches and let them sit for a few days in tightly sealed jars.

pomander bowls

Inexpensive, one-of-a-kind bowls often show up at yard sales (below, far right). Turn one into a gift by adding a pomander. These aromatic spheres are prepared by studding oranges with whole cloves, spaced evenly and as close together as possible (below, near right). Pomanders are used to scent closets and drawers. Finish the gift with ribbons and ornaments (below).

sachets

A potpourri sachet is that rare gift that caters to the sense of smell. Sachets are best known for making a room fresh and inviting, but they have many uses. Most shops that stock dried flowers and herbs also carry small muslin bags, similar to those shown at left. Fill these bags with fragrant flora such as (below, clockwise from top left) rose petals, white sage, cedar bits and tips, lavender, eucalyptus, juniper berries, and (center) orange peel.

PUTTING IT TOGETHER

By mixing and matching different ingredients, you can make a potpourri fragrance that is floral, spicy, citrusy, or fresh. Experiment with some of your favorite flowers and herbs, or try some of our ideas:

1. For a special holiday scent, mix evergreen trimmings, dried orange peel, bay leaves, cloves, and cinnamon.

2. For a lingerie drawer, mix rose petals, citrus peels and lavender.

3. For a man's drawer, mix red cedar branch tips, lavender and eucalyptus.

4. For a sleep sachet, mix lemon verbena, lavender, marjoram, and rose petals.

5. For a relaxing bathtub sachet, mix lemon verbena, chamomile and lime blossoms, and wrap in cheesecloth; the sachet should be tossed under running water.

Be sure to add a fixative such as orrisroot to your homemade potpourri to hold the delicate fragrance of your flowers and herbs and make them last. For each cup of potpourri that you make, sprinkle about a tablespoon of the fixative over the dry materials. Mix well with your fingers or a wooden spoon.

Two pairs of rolled candles are wrapped in silk tissue and tied with ribbon. The natural palette of beeswax can range from ivory to butter yellow to deep olive.

CANDLES

This simple gift creates a world of light, magic, elegance, and intimacy

There is nothing visually warmer on a cold winter night than candlelight.

Electric lights spread people out, but candle flame lures them in to a small circle, a charmed

sphere where they can talk in whispers and still be heard, where the rest of the world dissolves

in dark edges and shadow, and what is most important—each other—is the only thing visible.

Shut the overheads and light a beeswax taper and the room turns instantly amber,

and people draw close. The air becomes redolent with a faint fragrance of honey.

Christmas is a time for **candles,** for coming together. Make them as you wish:

hand-rolled, dipped, or molded; stamped or scented. But whichever way

you choose, once the candles have dried, they'll impart much more than merely light.

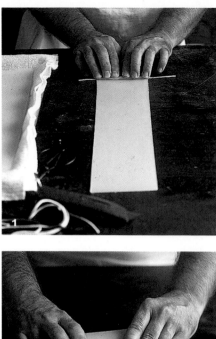

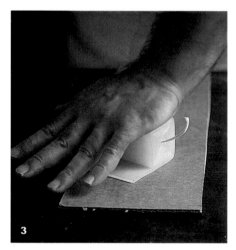

ROLLED

With the advent of mass-produced candles in the nineteenth century, candlemaking disappeared from the list of household chores. But machine-made candles don't have the sensuous shapes of dipped tapers or the lush colors of home-dyed and molded candles.

In recent years, hand candlemaking has reached the plane of both popular craft and high art. The tools and methods are almost as simple today as they were five thousand years ago. Candlemaking-supply houses and craft shops stock everything you need to create candles at home—paraffin, beeswax, wicking, molds, wax-dye pellets, and wax hardeners.

The candles on these pages are made from softened sheets of solid beeswax.

how to roll

Heat an electric griddle to 350 degrees or an oven to 250 degrees. If using a griddle, lay a sheet of wax on a piece of terry-cloth toweling that has been cut to size. Heat for three or four minutes. When sheet is warm and pliable, quickly remove and place on a work surface. To soften in an oven, place sheet on a towel-covered cookie sheet and warm for two minutes. Using a mat knife, cut the wax to the desired height of the candle.

1. Lay a length of wicking (slightly longer than the wax) along one end of the sheet.

2. Roll the wax, keeping the ends even.

3. To make a square candle, press down as you roll the wax until you have four flat sides.

ABOVE: An array of rolled candles, round and square, in bright and muted colors.

4. When the candle has reached desired dimensions, slice off excess wax with a sharp blade. For an outer skin of a different hue, roll the cooled candle in another sheet of softened wax.

5. To finish the candle and erase the seam, roll it quickly on a metal bar (available from scrap-metal dealers) that has been heated on the griddle or in the oven. To finish a square candle, press each side against the bar.

6. Smooth rough edges with a warm metal tool such as a palette knife or a trowel.

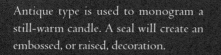

Antique type is used to monogram a still-warm candle. A seal will create an embossed, or raised, decoration.

DIPPED

Lean and graceful, these hand-dipped tapers
give off a soft, meditative glow.

how to dip

Two candles are dipped at once, one at either end of a wick.

Melt beeswax or paraffin in a double boiler. The container for the wax can be a candle-dipping pot or any pot tall enough to accommodate the length of candle you're making; it should be placed in a stockpot half full of water set over an electric burner on high heat. The temperature should remain below two hundred degrees on a candy thermometer. Because heated wax can ignite, never leave it unattended; lower heat immediately if you smell wax burning or if it starts to smoke. Two to three pounds of wax may require an hour or more to melt. The color can be deepened with shavings from a block of darker beeswax or wax-dye pellets.

ABOVE LEFT: As wax is melting, prepare wick: Cut a length of wicking that will leave enough room for dipping a candle on each end. Tie weights to wick ends—try fishing weights, metal nuts, or several pennies stuck together with bits of soft wax. Use fifteen-ply wicking for thin tapers, twenty-four-ply for candles thicker than half an inch.

ABOVE RIGHT: Test wax temperature and seal wick by dipping the ends, up to desired candle length, into melted wax. It should harden four seconds after wick is removed (at about 165 degrees). Holding wick at midpoint, re-dip ends into wax, then plunge candles into cold water. Repeat until they reach desired diameter.

RIGHT: Hang finished candles over a broom balanced on two chair backs, making sure candles don't touch. Let harden for a day in a cool, draft-free spot. With a mat knife, cut off weights and redip ends to finish taper bottoms.

BELOW: Finished dipped tapers hang from braided wicks.

99

MOLDED

Candlemaking-supply houses and craft shops offer a staggering array of metal candle molds—they usually come with instructions on what gauge wicking is required and how much wax is necessary. There are tiny votive cylinders and spheres as well as elegant obelisks, blocks, and oval shapes. Keep in mind that many candlemakers say that simple shapes display the various hues and textures of the wax most effectively.

BELOW AND MIDDLE RIGHT: An eclectic collection of molds provided the inspiration for these deep-hued candles.

TOP RIGHT: A simple mold made from a paper-towel tube will impress candles with a rough, granitelike surface. This bunch is tied together with antique monogrammed ribbon.

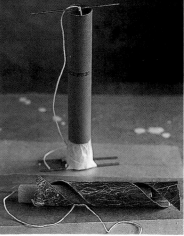

how to mold

Prepare a mold by fixing a length of wick to the bottom with a screw and a bit of putty. These will usually come packaged with the mold. Plumber's putty can be substituted for wick putty. Place a toothpick, pencil, or stick across the top of the mold. Pull the wick up the center of the mold and tie it to the stick.

1. Melt paraffin or beeswax in a double boiler according to the instructions for dipped candles. When wax has reached two hundred degrees on a candy thermometer, lower heat and add a hardening agent such as stearic acid or synthetic hardening crystals—most candlemakers prefer the crystals. Use one-half to one

BELOW: To give the candle a beveled edge, very quickly run the edges along a hot metal bar (as described in step 5 on page 96) or shave the edges off with a very sharp blade, such as an X-Acto knife.

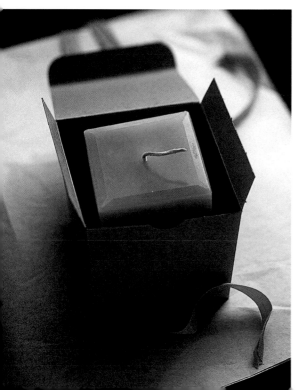

teaspoon of the crystals or three tablespoons of stearic acid per pound of wax.

2. To tint the melting wax, stir in bits of wax-dye pellets until dissolved. Test the color on a cookie sheet or with a cotton swab.

3. Pour the melted wax into prepared mold until it is an inch and a half below the rim.

4. Using pot holders, place the filled mold in a cold-water bath—a bucket works fine. The water should be level with the wax. Let the mold sit for about thirty minutes. As air bubbles rise to the top, a small well will form around the wick. Insert a long, thin instrument, such as a cake tester or knitting needle, into the well to allow air bubbles to escape, then fill the well three-quarters full with more melted wax. Repeat the process again after forty-five minutes, then remove the mold from the water bath. Allow mold to cool and harden for eight hours, turning it periodically to ensure even cooling.

5. Remove the wick screw and putty, then gently pull the candle from the mold. With a knife, even off the candle bottom, then polish it by rubbing any rough spots on a cookie sheet heated over a stove burner.

To make candles from a paper-towel tube (pictured on opposite page), secure a piece of wicking inside by tying it to a toothpick at each end of the tube. Close up one end of the tube using masking tape. Pour in melted wax and allow it to harden for six to eight hours. Then peel cardboard tubing off and finish the bottom as you would any other molded candle.

VOTIVES

Making votive candles is a good way to use up beeswax left over from other candlemaking projects. Votives make wonderful small gifts. They also create a dramatic lighting effect when lined up on a windowsill, mantel, or bookshelf.

LEFT: Many of us grew up drinking our milk out of jelly glasses. But using the jars that way neglects one of their most useful properties: the ability of their thick, tempered glass to withstand heat. Antique jelly jars (they often come with lids) are perfect vessels for scented candles.

BELOW LEFT: Small molds can also be used to make votives; do plenty so you'll always have some on hand.

BELOW: The warm glow of a candle becomes warmer still when it emanates from a ruddy terra-cotta pot.

how to make votives

ABOVE: To make jelly jar votives, begin by fixing a wick with a metal wick tab to the bottom of a jar using plumber's or wick putty; suspend the wick from a pencil laid across the top of the jar. Place some bleached beeswax (a pound fills four or five eight-ounce jars) in a double boiler and heat to 135 degrees (check with a candy thermometer). Remove wax from heat and stir in about fifty drops of a pure, oil-based plant essence such as lavender, sandalwood, or jasmine. (The exact amount will depend on the oil's intensity and your own preference.) Pour wax into the jars; set them in a water bath to cool. Add more wax as needed.

RIGHT: To make potted terra-cotta candles start with a collection of delicate three- or four-inch flowerpots from the garden shop or hardware store. Close the drainage hole with a penny or a bit of aluminum foil. In an old saucepan, melt a block of beeswax. Tie a six-inch length of medium-gauge wick (called "W-2") to a twig. Dip the entire wick in the wax and pull it straight. Suspend the wick in the center of the pot. Then pour a tablespoon of wax into the pot to secure the wick in the bottom and let harden for fifteen minutes. Fill the pot three-quarters full in three stages, allowing the wax to harden a bit after adding each portion. Remove the twig and trim the wick. You can add a jot of citronella, available at hardware stores, to the melted wax for bug-repellent outdoor candles.

To make molded votive candles (shown opposite, below left), follow the directions for melting wax on page 99. Pour melted wax into votive molds fitted with wick tabs—stiff wicks anchored to metal tabs placed directly in the bottom of the votive mold. These can be cooled in a shallow water bath and will harden in a few hours.

CANDLE TIPS

1. To prolong the burning life of candles, store them in the freezer until they are ready to be lit.

2. When making a candle, be sure to use a proper wick, not just a simple piece of string. The wick is braided in one direction to minimize dripping as the candle burns.

3. For a rolled candle, test out your design with a paper template before working in wax. Once the wax is cut, it's hard to correct mistakes.

4. To make those too-wide tapers fit into your favorite candlesticks, use a candle-sharpener—not a knife—to narrow the ends. The sharpener cuts smoothly and in a perfect circle.

5. To hold a tipping candle in its candlestick, drip a bit of melted wax in the bottom and immediately insert the taper. The wax will harden and hold the candle upright.

6. To blow out candles without splattering wax, place your finger in front of the flame and blow gently.

7. To remove wax from a linen tablecloth, first rub the area with an ice cube to freeze the wax. Then, using your fingernail or a spatula, gently scrape as much of the hardened wax from the fabric as you can. Next, place the tablecloth on an inverted colander in the sink with the stained area in the center. Pour boiling water over the stain to melt the remaining wax.

WRAPPING

A perfectly turned-out package is alive with possibility and personality

Part of the fun of receiving gifts is unwrapping them, unlocking,

ribbon by ribbon, layer by layer, the shrouded casement and finding the secret at

its core. But for some people, gift **wrapping** is as much a mystery as what

the package is hiding. The folding and pleating and cutting can seem

impossibly difficult. But the truth is that anyone can learn to make

perfect packages. In this chapter, we'll show you how to fold and

wrap ends elegantly and neatly, as well as how to make perfect bows. Once the skill is acquired,

you can experiment with different materials and themes, putting your own

personal stamp on the present from the outset. Ribbons can be made of

moiré, grosgrain, velvet, or even paper. Corrugated cardboard, cellophane, vellum,

rice or tissue paper can enclose the gift. And not all containers need to be boxes.

We'll show different ways to wrap soft gifts, such as scarves and ties.

Gift tags have possibilities, too. Use our suggestions or create

your own special wrappings. Once you've mastered

the science, you will have not only boxes beneath

the tree, but also works of art.

OPPOSITE: The ribbon (above) was stamped with a star pattern cut into a pencil eraser; dots on paper are hand-painted. A metallic marker was used to write on neon-colored price tags (below), available from office-supply stores.

THIS PAGE: Japanese rice paper comes in a variety of subtle patterns. The antique silver ribbon is tied with silver ornament balls.

THE PERFECT PACKAGE

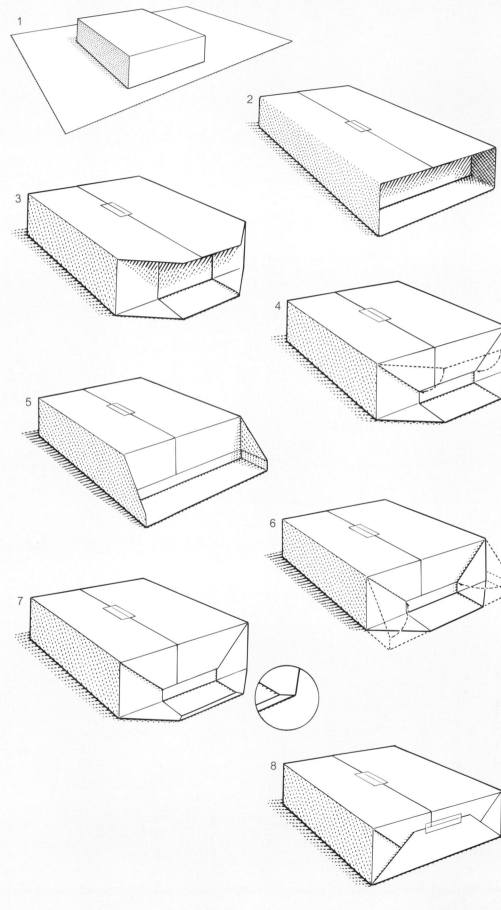

wrapping the ends

Once you master the basics, putting together a package is really quite simple. Here, we show two ways of folding the ends, both of which create an elegant finish. Before you cut the paper, roughly fold it over the gift to make sure you've got a big enough piece.

1. Place the box or gift upside down on the wrapping paper, so the seam will be on the bottom.

2. Bring the paper around the box and tape. The paper should be pulled taut.

3. Fold in the sides, creasing around the box edges.

4. Fold down the top flap, creasing around edge, then bring up the bottom flap. Seal with tape. Repeat on other end of package.

5. For an alternate finish, fold down top flap. Crease sides.

6. Fold in side flaps and crease.

7. Fold over a small bit of bottom flap. This will give the end a smooth line.

8. Seal end with tape.

tying the bow

This is Martha's favorite bow (opposite), and it's foolproof. Loosely wrap the ribbon around the package you'll be tying to get an idea of the required length (for a very large bow or long tails, allow more ribbon). Wrap the ribbon around the package, making sure ribbon is pulled taut.

1. Form ends into two equal loops with about ten inches of ribbon between them.

2. Cross the right loop over the left.

3, 4. Knot the loops by pushing right loop behind left, under, and through the hole.

5. Pull the knot tight.

6. Adjust the loops and tails until they are the same size. Notch the ends, if desired.

Ribbon is one of the elements that can give packages a distinctive look. Monochromatic ribbon and paper create a sophisticated package, while contrasting ribbon and paper make a bold statement. Novelty-patterned ribbon adds a whimsical touch. Different kinds of ribbon create different effects. MOIRÉ ribbon is stiff and substantial, with a shimmering watermark finish. It's especially suitable for making bows. GROSGRAIN and FAILLE, with their crossgrain ribs, are probably the best-known ribbons; their weave gives them a subtle elasticity. ORGANDY is sheer and can be either floppy or crisp. It gives a package a delicate look, and should be used with a wrapping paper that won't overwhelm it. The plush pile of VELVET creates real heft; this type of ribbon works best on large packages. SATIN is the most fluid and luxurious of ribbon materials. TAFFETA ribbon is very finely woven silk or rayon, and is crisp and delicate. PAPER ribbon gives a package a rustic look, and is often wired for easy manipulating. PICOT EDGING (sometimes called feather edging) is delicately looped threadwork that appears on all types of ribbon.

TISSUE PAPER

THIS PAGE: A pine-tree profile cut into gold tissue paper folds back to reveal a layer of silvery-blue tissue. First, wrap a box in the tissue; then fold gold paper around it, leaving impressions where the edges and corners should be; remove. Outline half of a tree on the center of the wrong side of the gold paper, cut along the outer edge with an X-Acto knife, and fold outward. Wrap package with gold paper, centering tree.

OPPOSITE: When opened, a plain box reveals its dot-stamped lid and matching tissue.

STAMPING

printed paper

Create your own designs with stamps made from scratch (left). Erasers are versatile stamping tools because they can be cut cleanly and hold ink nicely. For large stamps, choose white-gum artist's erasers. Use aluminum cookie and vegetable cutters to cut out shapes: Sandwich the eraser and cutter between two pieces of wood or stiff cardboard and stand on top to exert enough pressure to cut the eraser. Paper printed with harlequin or leaf designs (below left and far left) is unusual and eye catching. To make imprints in an array of vivid colors, try using gouache paints (below), available at art-supply stores. The paints are water-soluble, opaque, and quick-drying. To stamp with gouache, thin a teaspoon-size bit with a drop of water on an old cookie sheet, plate, or small piece of glass. For even application, roll the gouache onto the stamp with a sponge roller.

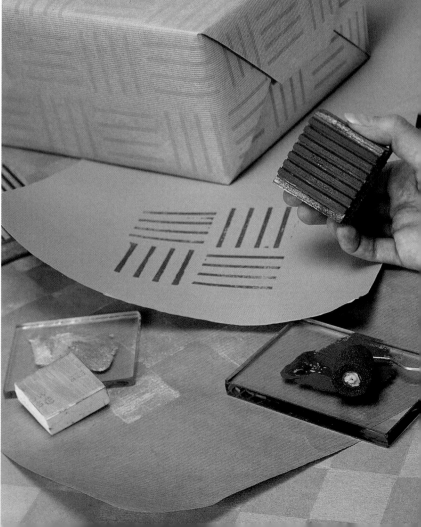

ribbons

ABOVE: A good ribbon can dress up a plain box all by itself. To customize cloth or paper ribbon, stamp it as you would a sheet of paper. Lay the ribbon flat and weight the ends to hold it in place, then stamp as desired, using acrylic or gouache paints as ink. Satin and taffeta ribbons take stamps especially well. Pencil erasers are the perfect scale for stamping ribbons. They make great dots without any carving; to cut out a design, draw on it first, then slice down into eraser with an X-Acto knife.

RIGHT: Rubber tubing, available at hardware stores, and metallic gold ink were used to stamp the paper ribbon; you can experiment with the various circumferences available. The wire edges of the paper ribbon allow it to be trained into any shape, with fingers or an object. The snail-like curl (above right) was formed around a pencil, and then attached to the package with sealing wax.

SOFT PACKAGING

The wrappings shown on these pages are suitable for flat, soft gifts like a tie or wallet.

ABOVE: Tissue-wrapped gifts wear sheaths of contrasting papers. The 5"-square flat package, right, is encased in gold tissue; a 7"-square piece of green rag paper is wrapped around the box so that its corners just barely meet at the center front. A bay leaf painted gold is secured with paper glue. Beside it, a 6"-by-4" lilac package is encased in vellum, cut into a 6"-by-8" rectangle; black satin ribbon is laced through holes punched into the vellum where edges meet.

LEFT AND BELOW: To make a pouch, you'll need a sheet of paper several times larger than the gift. With the paper's length running horizontally and its wrong side up, fold a vertical pleat in the middle. Fold over one side to cover pleat line; crease. Fold over the other side to cover the first and crease. Open folds and place gift in center. Refold. Fold remaining sides to enclose gift and crease. Tuck one end inside the other to secure.

Any plain paper bag can become fancy wrapping with a closure of decorative machine stitching. After placing a gift inside, fold the bag closed. Using silk buttonhole thread and a No. 16 needle, sew the bag with a bead, scallop, or zigzag stitch. For variation, leave thread ends long or add a second, parallel line of stitching. For a dressier bag, cut a decorative edge with pinking shears. Bags can also be embellished with labels or stamps.

cellophane bags

For tall gifts or a number of small trinkets, a cellophane bag, above, lined with brightly colored tissue paper, is ideal. Identify the recipient by attaching an initial letter and jingle bells.

corrugated paper

The bottom gift, left, was wrapped in gold tissue, then enclosed in a sleeve of corrugated paper cinched with 5"-wide crimson antique taffeta ribbon, and tied with thin black ribbon. To make the package with eye-shaped ends, cut a 12"-by-10" rectangle from corrugated paper. With corrugated side down, make a lengthwise fold 3½" from one side and another 2½" from the other. Fold sides inward to make a flattened tube. Trace a convex curve at each end, using the edge of a plate. With an X-Acto knife, cut along curves through all layers and unfold. On smooth side, use a pencil to complete each curve in an eye shape 1¾" tall at center. Push down firmly to score paper. Fold sides around wrapped gift, then fold ends inward along scored lines. Wind ribbon around package; secure with a hat pin.

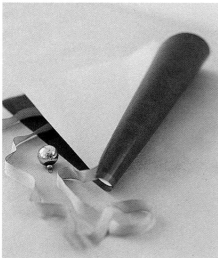

paper cones

The cone, left, was made from a 12"-by-12" square of card stock and a square of German waxed paper ⅛" larger on all sides. Tape a 72" length of seam binding to one corner of the card stock; this will be the point of the cone. Roll both sheets into a slender cone, and secure with tape. Stuff the point of the cone with tissue; place gift inside. Fold top flap forward to make a lid. Wrap seam binding up back, over top, and down front, encircling cone twice. Tie ribbon ends together at center front, looping a glass ball through knot.

POTATO PRINTS

Potatoes are wonderful mashed, baked, scalloped, or fried, but they have a less conventional use, as printing stamps for personalized gift cards and tags.

To make a potato print, cut a spud (any variety will do) in half and draw a shape onto the flesh with a pencil. Then, using an X-Acto knife or a jackknife with a thin blade, carve around the outline and cut away the background of the pencil design to a depth of one-quarter inch. Thin gouache paints (available at art-supply stores) with a little water, then apply the paint directly onto the design with a brush or dip the potato into a dish of paint as though using a stamp pad. Finally, press the potato onto blank cards as many times as the color holds. Each print will look unique and slightly irregular, its own work of art. To make the card into a gift tag, punch a hole in the corner of the card with a nail, and attach coordinating or contrasting embroidery floss or raffia for ties.

TAGS & CARDS

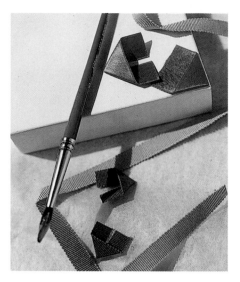

LEFT: In a season rife with flamboyant gift wraps, a simple card on a basic box can be a welcome change. To make the "David" tag , cut 2" snippets of satin ribbon, fold into points (above), iron flat, then glue onto the box's corners. To make the "Susan"tag, fold and iron a piece of grosgrain ribbon into a rectangle. Glue the top and bottom to the box; leave sides loose so you can slide in a card.

OPPOSITE: The sentiments on holiday gift tags can fill a booklet or be abbreviated to a single initial (top left). Brightly patterned Japanese kozo paper lends color to both. To make the letters, back the lightweight kozo paper with white card stock using Spray-Mount, an adhesive available at art-supply stores. Spritz the adhesive lightly over the white paper, and smooth the kozo paper over it. When dry, trace the letters on the white side using a stencil (placed backward, so the letters will read right-way-around on the printed side), and cut out with an X-Acto knife. The tiny book is made from a 6"-by-2" rectangle of Japanese kozo paper and two sheets of white paper cut to the same size. Bind the booklet with a single stitch through the spine, made with an ordinary needle and cotton thread. Peg-alphabet stamps (top right), available from art-supply stores, personalize simple aluminum-edged tags. Punch a hole in each tag, and print out a greeting using the stamps. Then string ⅛"-wide silver ribbon through the holes, and secure the tags to the gift. The white disk can also be colored to match the wrapping or ribbon (bottom right).

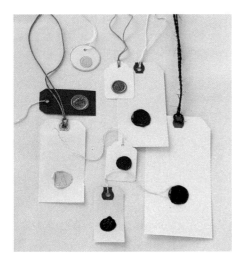

ABOVE: Stationery stores carry small cards and cardboard mailing tags. An embosser can imprint a star, snowflake, or initial on your tags. Sealing wax and stamps will personalize a heavy-duty mail tag. (Melt the sealing wax by holding it over a slow-burning votive candle, using a spoon to catch wax. Pour melted wax from the spoon directly onto tag, then stamp.)

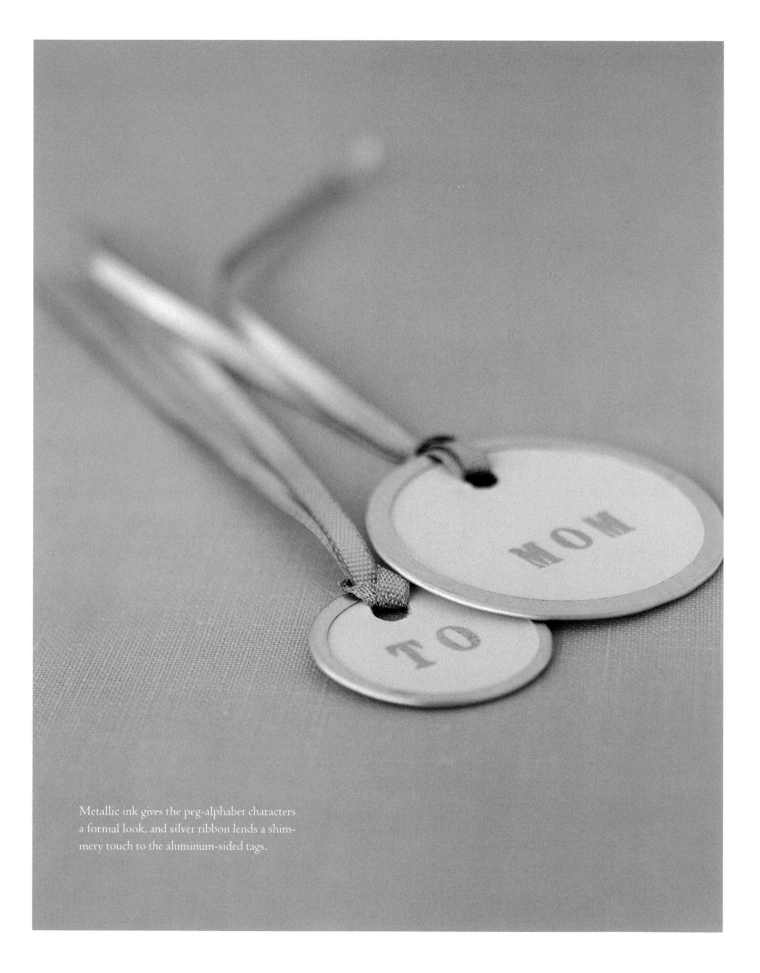

Metallic ink gives the peg-alphabet characters
a formal look, and silver ribbon lends a shim-
mery touch to the aluminum-sided tags.

Seashell images from vintage engravings are rubbed with metallic pigments to decorate gift tags. Use a color photocopier to transfer an engraving onto stationery paper. The copy should be in black only. You'll get a slightly raised image, which allows the color to adhere to the pattern. Gently rub the page with transparent, iridescent oil pastels. When the pastel is lightly rubbed off with tissue, it remains stuck to the pattern of the engraving, leaving behind a burnished finish.

VELLUM & GLASSINE

Vellum gives an elegant finish to cards and tags. To make the photograph cards, use reprints of a favorite snapshot and creamy card stock or blank cards from a stationery store. Cover the photograph with a sheet of translucent vellum, attaching it with a ribbon looped through two punched holes, or glue your picture to the inside leaf of a card and, using an X-Acto knife, cut a peek-a-boo window in the front leaf. A card can also double as an ornament when you attach a wire hook to the corner. Fasten your photo to the card stock by slipping the corners through four slits cut with a knife. You can write a message on the cards, or let the picture say it all.

BELOW LEFT: Stamped with woodblock letters and sewn onto a white paper bag, a sheet of vellum acts as a gift label. Leaves and coins are visible inside the other bags.

BELOW: Glassine has a lovely milk-white translucence. This gift tag is made from Color Aid, a painted artists' paper, softened inside a glassine envelope. Cut the card ⅛" smaller than the envelope on all sides, trace an initial on the back side using a stencil, and cut out the letter with an X-Acto knife. Glassine envelopes and sheets are inexpensive and are available from stamp-collectors' shops.

OPPOSITE: Glassine, which is nearly impermeable to grease, can be used to package seeds or food gifts, as a top layer for a package, or to encase photographs and gift tags.

OUTDOOR DISPLAYS

At the holidays, exteriors should be as cheery as interiors, with decorations for all the world to see

The Christmas tree, the ornaments, the stockings are

all gifts for family and friends to enjoy. But outdoor displays—

lights, porch swags, tassels, garlands, wreaths—are presents to your neighbors.

They are a way of imparting a holiday spirit to the surrounding community,

a way of sharing a ritual with people you may never even meet. Seen from the street by strollers,

or from a passing car, these decorations are a pleasure to behold,

especially up north when all the green has gone from the land. That's why

we dress up the house, draping it with fir tassels and flickering lights, with

pinecones and garlands of boxwood and berries.

Outdoor lighting can be expressive and sculptural, rather than dependent on architectural forms like house lines and branches. This tree is accessorized with bright, jewelrylike ornaments created from balled grapevine.

LIGHTS

During the winter months, a little light goes a long way. Even a strand, like the proverbial string of pearls, will stand out against the blackness. But bear in mind that you don't have to work in all white to be tasteful. Color can often achieve softer, simpler effects. There's a lot you can do with white, though: White bulbs are available in clear and glass, large and small sizes, and different shapes, from globe to candelabra taper. Variation is what's essential: You might also try lighting different parts of your display at different times, rather than all the lights all the time, to create a change of scene over the season.

ABOVE: Bulb reflectors, plastic collars that fit between bulb and socket, come in a variety of colors and different cut-crystal patterns. Star-shaped lights can achieve the same refracted effect.

OPPOSITE: An arbor strung with all-white lights, in different bulb sizes, shapes, and wattages, arcs across a pine-needle front path like dazzling lightning.

grapevine clusters
Martha Stewart wraps white minilights around grapevine balls of different sizes and nests them in a tree. The balls can be purchased at a garden center (see The Guide). Be sure to use outdoor lights, which won't freeze or shatter. And as an extra precaution, wrap strand connections securely in wide electrical tape. Also, use heavy-duty outdoor extension cords to run electricity from the house to the lighting.

spot touches

LEFT: The tree is ablaze with brilliant red lights, accented by the occasional white bulb. On a house, single-color strands create a more graphic silhouette than a confetti of colors.

BELOW: Minilights are bundled into knots with elastic ponytail holders (left) to form ornaments for a front-door wreath and adjacent garland (right). The garland has multi-colored glass balls illuminated with strategically placed white lights.

OPPOSITE: A small cove of trees at the corner of a house glows with harborlike lights. One color was used for each tree.

GREENERY

Why stop at the halls? This season, deck the whole house with boughs of greenery. Creating your own decorations from holly, boxwood, and pine isn't as easy as just hanging a wreath on the front door, but the effort yields beautiful results. Before you begin work, assess your home's strongest features. Then design trimmings to accent them: Swag pillars with garlands, hang oversized tassels from window pediments, thatch a gabled wall. With some basic equipment—chicken wire, florist's wire, rope, pliers, a staple gun, wire cutters, and a good pair of work gloves— you'll soon have your house looking as jolly outside as it does within.

holly and nandina wreath

This large, outdoor wreath is made on a plywood form. Have a lumberyard cut a wood frame in the size and shape you wish. Cut holly and nandina branches into four-to-six-inch lengths, stripping leaves from the nandina. (You can use any berried branch; nandina is widely available, and its berries dry well.) Staple holly to frame, covering cut ends. Staple nandina branches among the holly.

NANDINA BERRIES

SPRUCE

SPRUCE CONES

LARCH CONES

DOUGLAS FIR

ELVIS

PINE

CEDAR

HOLLY

CEDAR

WHITE PINE

TRUE FIR

BOXWOOD

MIXED GREENS

In addition to the greenery pictured above, other greens suitable for making decorations are English ivy, dusty miller (in places where it's hardy all winter), salal, and evergreen ferns. Most of the projects described on these pages require more than an armload of greenery, so check with florists, nurseries, and Christmas-tree dealers to see what's in stock.

A Scotch-pine garland punctuated with pinecone rosettes is draped around a snow-bound porch, casting stark shadows.

boxwood garland

To make a garland for a window or door (above), measure enough rope to fit around the frame. Cut tips of boxwood branches into six-to-eight-inch lengths. Bind a cluster of clippings to the rope with florist's wire at the cut ends. Wire another cluster a few inches farther along so that leaves cover the cut ends of previous cluster. Continue until rope is covered. Hammer four-inch nails (right) at the corners of the window or door. Drape garland over the upper two nails, snapping branches to angle at corners. Secure with florist's wire. For the window, overlap ends where they meet; bind with the wire.

pinecone rosette

The rosette, left, begins with a wreath made from a two-foot branch of Scotch pine looped in a circle and secured with florist's wire. Trim branches bearing pinecones to fit into center of wreath (like spokes or side by side, depending on branches), and wire to wreath. Add more pinecones to center by wrapping wire around base of each cone and binding it to a branch.

evergreen tassels

To make the tassel above, roll a piece of 12"-wide chicken wire into a tapered sleeve. Crush a second piece into a ball. Secure ball to narrow end of sleeve with florist's wire. Thread one prong of a bare, forked branch through top of ball, and wire it to other prong. Hide bound ends inside ball. Suspend form from this hanger. Beginning at top, poke six-to-eight-inch fir branches into ball, making a full puff.

Stuff three-foot fir branches up into sleeve (pushing cut ends into ball) until it is full. From outside, push more branches up into ball flat against sleeve. Wrap florist's wire around sleeve from top to bottom. Push cut ends of slightly shorter branches into sleeve, adding more toward bottom. Wrap tassel loosely with florist's wire. Repeat process three more times, using shorter branches for each layer, binding each layer except the final one with wire. With clippers, carefully trim the bottom, sides, and ball.

131

porch swag
Giant tassels of balsam and Douglas fir hang from pedimented windows. The finished tassels should be thick and shaggy.

PHOTOGRAPHY

william abranowicz
pages 122, 128-133, 141, 143.

carlton davis
page 84.

reed davis
pages 8 (middle right), 14, 16 (second from top), 17 (bottom left), 18, 26, 27 (bottom), 42-43, 46-51,
71 (top right), 83 (top and middle right), 86, 91, 92 (top), 100 (bottom right), 102 (bottom right), 103 (middle column),
117 (bottom left), 120 (top), 121, 136, 137 (right),139, back cover (bottom center).

john dugdale
pages 9 (middle left), 17, 27 (bottom right), 67 (top left), 68.

todd eberle
pages 15 (right), 16 (bottom left and right).

stewart ferebee
cover, page 10, back cover (top right).

dana gallagher
pages 4, 8 (left), 27 (top left), 28, 52 (top), 62, 74, 90, 95, 100 (top), 102 (top left), 103 (left and bottom right), 138.

gentl & hyers
pages 93, 104 (right), 105, 108, 112 (top right), 114, 117-119, 120 (bottom right), 141 (left).

ian gittler
pages 54 (bottom), 55 (left), 87 (bottom).

thibault jeanson
pages 9 (right), 82, 83 (bottom left and middle), 123-127, 135, back cover (top left).

stephen lewis
pages 13, 16 (second from bottom), 22 (top left, bottom), 23, 24, 65, 71 (bottom left and right),
87 (top), 89 (top), 92 (bottom row), 115-116, back cover (center left).

victoria pearson
pages 3, 6, 8 (right), 12, 15 (top and bottom left), 16 (top left and right), 20-21, 22 (top right), 25, 29, 53, 54 (top left and right),
55 (right), 58-61, 70, 71 (top left), 72 (top and bottom right), 73, 107, back cover (bottom right).

jose picayo
pages 5, 19, 52 (bottom), 66 (top left and bottom right), 66, 67, 69, 72 (bottom left).

maria robledo
pages 1, 8 (middle left), 9 (left), 30-41, 75-79, 81, 88, 89 (bottom row), 94, 96-101, 102 (bottom left),
137 (left), 140, 144, back cover (top center, bottom left).

chris sanders
page 85.

victor schrager
pages 2, 9 (middle right), 64, 104 (left), 109-111, 112 (bottom left and right),
113, 120 (bottom left), back cover (center right).

ILLUSTRATIONS

harry bates

THE GUIDE

Items pictured but not listed are from private collections. Addresses and telephone numbers of sources may change prior to publication, as may price and availability of any item.

WREATHS & SWAGS

Special thanks to L. Becker Flowers, 217 East 83rd Street, New York, NY 10028; 212-439-6001.

page 12

Silver balls (used in runner), $4.50 per dozen, *from D. Blümchen & Co., P.O. Box 1210-M, Ridgewood, NJ 07451-1210; 201-652-5595. Catalogue available.*

page 13

Eucalyptus leaves, $10 for 4 stems, *from U.S. Evergreen, 805 Sixth Avenue, New York, NY 10001; 212-741-5300.* **Antique metallic ribbon,** $10 to $25 per yard, *from Bell'occhio, 8 Brady Street, San Francisco, CA 94103; 415-864-4048.* **10" single-wire wreath frames,** $1 for 3, *from Galveston Wreath Co., 1124 25th Street, Galveston, TX 77550; 409-765-8597 or 800-874-8597. Catalogue, $5. Also available from Joe Makrancy's Garden and Floral Shop, 966 Kuser Road, Trenton, NJ 08619; 609-587-2543.*

pages 15, 16

22" oak-leaf wreath, $38, and **10" grape-**

vine sphere, $38 for kit of three spheres, or $58 for kit of three spheres and red plum leaves, *both from Green Valley Growers, 10450 Cherry Ridge Road, Sebastopol, CA 95472; 707-823-5583.*

pages 17, 18

2" flower picks, $1.29 per package; Oasis **floral foam,** $2.25 per brick; **chicken wire,** $3.50 for two 12"-by-12" sheets, *all from Dorothy Biddle Service, HC01 P.O. Box 900, Greeley, PA 18425; 717-226-3239.* **Custommade geometric topiaries,** prices upon request; **handmade earthenware pot,** $28, *both from L. Becker Flowers, 217 East 83rd Street, New York, NY 10028; 212-439-6001. Greenery available at nurseries nationwide.*

pages 17, 19

Sheet moss, $2.50 for ½ pound, $4.90 for 1 pound, *from Joe Makrancy's Garden and Floral Shop, 966 Kuser Road, Trenton, NJ 08619; 609-587-2543.* **U-shaped pins,** $1.49 for 50, *from Floracraft, P.O. Box 400, Ludington, MI 49431; 616-843-3401.* **Styrofoam balls** *available at Ben Franklin and craft stores nationwide.*

page 19

Pearl hat pins ($16 for 144 ($35 minimum order), *from Sheru Enterprises, 49 West 38th Street, New York, NY 10018; 212-730-0766.* **Lustregild gold enamel paint,** $5.95 for ½ pint, $10.45 for 1 pint, *from Albert Constantine & Son Inc., 2050 East Chester Road, Bronx, NY 10461; 800-223-8087.*

pages 20, 21

Living **succulent wreaths** and do-it-yourself **supplies,** *from Teddy Colbert's Garden, P.O. Box 9, Somis, CA 93066; 800-833-3981.*

pages 22, 23

Laurel leaves, $3 per pound, *available from U.S. Evergreen, 805 Sixth Avenue, New York, NY 10001; 212-741-5300.* **½" glass balls,** $4.50 for 12, *from D. Blümchen & Co., P.O. Box 1210-M, Ridgewood, NJ 07451-1210; 201-652-5595. Catalogue available.* **Antique metallic ribbon** (used on wreath), $10 to $25 per yard, *from Bell'occhio, 8 Brady Street, San Francisco, CA 94103; 415-864-4048.*

page 24

Velvet grape leaves, $36 for 12, *from Dulken*

& Derrick, 12 West 21st Street, New York, NY 10010; 212-929-3614. Metallic and colored-**glass balls,** $4.50 for 12, and **pipe cleaners,** $1 for 25, *both available from D. Blümchen & Co., P.O. Box 1210-M, Ridgewood, NJ 07451-1210; 201-652-5595. Catalogue available.*

pages 26, 27

Wreath forms, *from Galveston Wreath Co., 1124 25th Street, Galveston, TX 77550; 409-765-8597 or 800-874-8597. Catalogue, $5.* **Greenery** *available at nurseries nationwide.*

page 27

Fruited wreath, $65, *from Green Valley Growers, 10450 Cherry Ridge Road, Sebastopol, CA 95472; 707-823-5583.* **Pepperberry tree,** $225, *from Fantasia Floral Design, 201 East 74th Street, New York, NY 10021; 212-517-3458. Pepperberries also available at selected florists.* **Styrofoam cones** *available at crafts and art-supply stores.*

page 28

Rose-hip wreath, $30, *from Green Valley Growers, 10450 Cherry Ridge Road, Sebastopol, CA 95472; 707-823-5583.*

COOKIE BOXES

pages 30, 33

Military ribbon, from $5 per yard, *from Tinsel Trading Company, 47 West 38th Street, New York, NY 10018; 212-730-1030.*

pages 30, 33, 35, 39

Unbleached natural **parchment paper,** $3.95 for five 8"-by-15" sheets, *from Balducci's, 424 Sixth Avenue, New York, NY 10011; 212-673-2600 or 800-225-3822.*

pages 30, 33, 39

8" square baking tin, $13, *available from Dean & DeLuca, 560 Broadway, New York, NY 10012; 212-431-1691. Catalogue $2.50.*

pages 31, 36

Small ice-cream mold, $17.97, *from New York Cake & Baking Center, 56 West 22nd Street, New York, NY 10010; 212-675-2253 or 800-942-2539. Catalogue available.* **Gauzy silver ribbon,** $10 to $25 per yard, *from Bell'occhio, 8 Brady Street, San Francisco, CA 94103; 415-864-4048.*

page 32

Half-moon pudding molds, $16.99 each, *from New York Cake & Baking Center, 56 West 22nd*

Street, New York, NY 10010; 212-675-2253 or 800-942-2539. *Catalogue available.* **Moiré ribbon,** $10 per yard for 4" width, *from Bell'occhio, 8 Brady Street, San Francisco, CA 94103; 415-864-4048.* ¼" linen **bookbinding tape,** $3.15 per roll, *from Talas, 568 Broadway, New York, NY 10012; 212-219-0770. Catalogue $4.*

page 33

Jute string, $7.95 per 1-pound reel, *from BZI Distributors, 105 Eldridge Street, New York, NY 10002; 212-966-6690 ($25 minimum).*

page 34

Unsweetened coconut, $1.75 for 5 ounces, *available from Dean & DeLuca, 560 Broadway, New York, NY 10012; 212-431-1691. Catalogue $2.50. Also available from health-food stores.*

page 35

Fluted pudding mold, $18, *from Dean & DeLuca, see above.*

page 36

Headband tape (on tallest mold), $1.80 per yard, *from Talas, 568 Broadway, New York , NY 10012; 212-219-0770. Catalogue $5.* **Military trim** (above headband tape), *from $5 per yard, from Tinsel Trading Company, 47 West 38th Street, New York, NY 10018; 212-730-1030.* **Checkered ribbon,** $1.59 per yard for woven variety, 98¢ per yard for printed, *from*

M&J Trimming, 1008 Sixth Avenue, New York, NY 10018; 212-391-9072.

pages 36, 39

⅛" **rickrack trim,** 25¢ per yard, *from Tinsel Trading Company, 47 West 38th Street, New York, NY 10018; 212-730-1030.*

pages 36, 40

Aluminum art-supply box, $25.20, *from New York Central Art Supply, 62 Third Avenue, New York, NY 10003; 212-473-7705 or 800-950-6111 (outside NYC).*

page 37

Brioche mold (in front), $2.75 to $12, depending on size, *from Dean & DeLuca, 560 Broadway, New York, NY 10012; 212-431-1691. Catalogue $2.50.*

page 38

Pullman loaf pan, $24.50 for 16" by 4", *from Broadway Panhandler, 477 Broome Street, New York, NY 10013; 212-966-3434.* Antique chartreuse **taffeta ribbon,** $16 per yard, *from Bell'occhio, 8 Brady Street, San Francisco, CA 94103; 415-864-4048.* Wide **indigo ribbon,** $10 to $15 per yard, *from Hyman Hendler & Sons, 67 West 38th Street, New York, NY 10018; 212-840-8393.* Antique **silver cord,** from $1.50 per yard, *from Tinsel Trading Company, 47 West 38th Street, New York, NY 10018; 212-730-1030.*

STOCKINGS

page 42

Purple faille-back satin ribbon (for cuff), $12.50 per yard; **rust satin-back velvet ribbon,** $9 per yard, *both from Hyman Hendler & Sons, 67 West 38th Street, New York, NY 10018; 212-840-8393. Ribbons also from Britex Fabrics, 146 Geary Street, San Francisco, CA 94108; 415-392-2910.* **Brick rayon velvet** (for body), $15.95 per yard, *from B&J Fabrics, 263 West 40th Street, New York, NY 10018; 212-354-8150.* **Antique knots,** $2.98 each, *from M&J Trimmings, 1008 Sixth Avenue, New York, NY 10018; 212-391-9072.*

pages 43, 51

Classic teddy bears by Steiff USA. *Call 800-779-6433 for nearest retailer.* **Bone-white Tempora felt** (for body), $24.75 per yard, *from Central/Shippee Inc., P.O. Box 135, Bloomingdale, NJ 07403; 201-838-1100.* **Hat fur felt** (for tree and flower details), $12.50 per hood (colors), $15.50 per hood (white), *from Manny's Millinery Supply, 26 West 38th Street, New York, NY 10018; 212-840-2235.* **Antique buttons,** starting at $2.50 per dozen (limited supply), *from Tinsel Trading, 47 West 38th Street, New York, NY 10018; 212-730-1030.*

page 46

Monogram stockings: Trim (for lettering), 25¢ per yard, *from Tinsel Trading Co., 47 West 38th Street, New York, NY 10018; 212-730-1030.* **Brown wool-cashmere blanket wool** (for cuff), **green wool-cashmere blanket**

wool (for body), both $79.95 per yard; **brown wool-cashmere blanket wool** (for cuff), $79.95 per yard, **camel lamb's-wool blanket wool** (for body), $39.95 per yard, *all from B&J Fabrics, 263 West 40th Street, New York, NY 10018; 212-354-8150.*
Multicolor stockings: Brown cashmere blanket wool (for cuff), $125 per yard, **orange wool-cashmere blanket wool** (for body), **green wool-cashmere blanket wool** (for heel and toe), **brown wool-cashmere blanket wool** (for cuff), **green wool-cashmere blanket wool** (for body), all $79.95 per yard, *all from B&J Fabrics, see above.*
Jester-cuff stockings: Bone-white wool-cashmere blanket wool (for cuff), $79.95 per yard; **navy cashmere blanket wool** (for body), $125 per yard, *both from B&J Fabrics, see above.* **Gold and silver jingle bells,** price varies with size, *from Sheru, 49 West 38th Street, New York, NY 10018; 212-730-0766.* **Brown wool-cashmere blanket wool** (for cuff), $39.95 per yard; **brown blanket wool** (for body), $29.95; *both from B&J Fabrics, see above.*

page 47

Silk taffeta (for cuff), $42.95 per yard; iridescent **blue-black and brown silk organza** (for body), $32.95 per yard, *both from B&J Fabrics, 263 West 40th Street, New York, NY 10018; 212-354-8150.* **Taffeta-back velvet ribbon,** $1.50 per yard, *from Hyman Hendler & Sons, 67 West 38th Street, New York, NY 10018; 212-840-8393.* **Chocolate gold coins,** $12 per pound, *from Li-Lac Chocolates Inc., 120 Christopher Street, New York, NY 10014; 212-242-7374.* German **colored**

pencils, $2 each, *from Terra Verde, 120 Wooster Street, New York, NY 10012; 212-925-4533.* Maple-sugar leaves *by Maple Grove Farms of Vermont Inc.,* $1.95, *from Dean & DeLuca, 800-221-7714.*

pages 48 to 50

Black Tempora felt (for body), $24.60 per yard, *from Central/Shippee Inc., P.O. Box 135, Bloomingdale, NJ 07403; 201-838-1100.* Hat fur felt (for flowers), $12.50 per hood (colors), $15.50 per hood (white), *from Manny's Millinery Supply, 26 West 38th Street, New York, NY 10018; 212-840-2235.*

page 51

Bakelite buttons, *from* $1.50 to $20 *each, from Tender Buttons, 143 East 62nd Street, New York, NY 10021; 212-758-7004; and 946 North Rush Street, Chicago, IL 60611; 312-337-7033. Also from Gordon Button Co., 222 West 38th Street, New York, NY 10018; 212-921-1684.* "Navaho" Tempora felt, $24.60 *per yard, from Central/Shippee Inc., P.O. Box 135, Bloomingdale, NJ 07403; 201-838-1100.* Candy pencils *by Churchill's of London,* $6.95 *for 10, from Dean & DeLuca, 800-221-7714.*

ORNAMENTS

pages 52, 59, 66 to 69

Dragées, $20 *per pound, from New York Cake & Baking Center, 56 West 22nd Street, New York, NY 10010; 212-675-2253 or 800-942-2539. Catalogue available.*

pages 52, 67

Knobby white urchins, $1, pink urchins, 39¢,

green urchins, 39¢, *all from the Shell Man, P.O. Box 1917, Key Largo, FL 33037; 305-451-0767.*

pages 53, 54

Giant handmade copper and brass cookie cutters, $65 *each, from Naiad and Walter Einsel Design, 26 Morningside Drive South, Westport, CT 06880; 203-226-0709.* 5"-wide satin ribbon, $12 *per yard, from Bell'occhio, 8 Brady Street, San Francisco, CA 94103; 415-864-4048.*

page 54

Ateco Spectrum food coloring, $1.26 to $1.56 per ounce depending on color, *from August Thomsen Corp; call 800-645-7170 for nearest dealer.*

page 55 to 57

Gingerbread-house *design adapted from Julboken, published by ICA Bokförlag (Västerås, Sweden, 1986).*

pages 58 to 61

Assorted millinery fruits, $9 to $15 *per bunch, from Bell'occhio, 8 Brady Street, San Francisco, CA 94103; 415-864-4048.* 2"-wide luminescent organdy ribbon, *by Midori Inc., 1432 Elliott Avenue West, Seattle, WA 98119. Call 206-282-3595 or 800-659-3049 for retail information.* Brass-mesh leaves, *special order from Dulken & Derrick Inc., 12 West 21st Street, New York, NY 10010; 212-929-3614.* Rattlebox beans, $3.75 *for about 35, from the Galveston Wreath Company, 1124 25th Street, Galveston, TX 77550; 409-765-8597.*

page 62

Antique metallic ribbon, $5 to $30 *per yard, from Hyman Hendler & Sons, 67 West 38th Street, New York, NY 10018; 212-840-8393.*

page 64

Ornaments from: *Barbara Trujillo Antiques, 2466 Main Street-Montauk Highway, Bridgehampton, NY 11932; 516-537-3838.* J. Goldsmith Antiques, *1924 Polk Street, San Francisco, CA 94109; 415-771-4055.* Kelter Malcé Antiques, *74 Jane Street, New York, NY 10014; 212-675-7380.* Linda Rosen Antiques *at the Tomato Factory Annex, Hopewell, NJ 08525; 609-466-9833.* Main Street Antiques, *156 Main Street, Flemington, NJ 08822; 908-788-6767.* U.S.E.D., *17 Perry Street, New York, NY 10014; 212-627-0730.* Feather trees *from Barbara Trujillo Antiques, see above.* Wooden-block tree stand, *custom-made by Christopher M. Cavallaro; 212-475-4371.*

page 65

Styrofoam cones *available at craft stores.*

pages 66 to 69

Blue starfish, $2.50 ($3 bleached), Pacific starfish, 60¢ to $1.50, auger shells, $2 *per pound,* polished trochus shells, $1, turban

shells, *from* 15¢, *all from the Shell Man, P.O. Box 1917, Key Largo, FL 33037; 305-451-0767.* Ruffled clamshells *from* $4, *from Blooming Shells, Main Street, Sag Harbor, NY 11963; 516-725-4428.*

page 66

Metal beads, $2.49 for 100 ($25 minimum), *from Shipwreck Beads, 2727 Westmoor Court, Olympia, WA 98502; 206-866-4061.*

pages 70, 71

Assorted birds, 75¢ to $3.25 *each, and* red velvet ribbon, $3.90 to $5.90 *per bolt (25 yards), from Angray Merchandising (Fantastico), 559 6th Street, San Francisco, CA 94103; 415-982-0680.*

page 71

Pinecones, $4.95 for 5-to-6-ounce sack, *from Galveston Wreath Co., 1124 25th Street, Galveston, TX 77550; 409-765-8597.*

pages 72, 73

Pinecones, freeze-dried roses, *and* seedpods *available from Wildflowers of Princeton Junction, 315 Cranbury Road, P.O. Box 726, Princeton Junction, NJ 08550; 609-275-6060 or 800-999-4459.* (*Iris and poppy pods,* $10 *per bunch;* nigella *and* cockscomb, $15 *per bunch;* rose hips *and* small pinecones, $20 *per bag;* large pinecones, $40 *per gross.*) Dremel Moto-Tool drill, *from Dremel, 4915 21st Street, Racine, WI 53406; call 800-437-3635 for catalogue and prices.*

page 72

Pearl hat pins, $16 for 144 ($35 minimum order), *from Sheru Enterprises, 49 West 38th Street, New York, NY 10018; 212-730-0766.*

GIFTS

page 74

Gift boxes, *from* $2 to $12, *from Party Bazaar, Cross County Shopping Center, Yonkers, NY 10704; 914-965-1465.* Tissue paper *by Crystal Tissue Co., at party-goods stores nationwide.* Crimson and taffeta ribbons, $22 to $32 *per yard, from Bell'occhio, 8 Brady Street, San Francisco, CA 94103; 415-864-4048.* Other ribbons *from Hyman Hendler & Sons, 67 West 38th Street, New York, NY 10018; 212-840-8393; and Britex Fabrics, 146 Geary Street, San Francisco, CA 94108; 415-392-2910.*

pages 75 to 77

Green moriki paper, $6.35 *per sheet, from Kate's Paperie, 8 West 13th Street, New York, NY 10011; 212-633-0570.* Gold washi paper, $7.70 *per sheet, from New York Central Art Supply, 62 Third Avenue, New York, NY 10003; 212-473-7705 or*

800-950-6111 (*outside NYC*). **Gold ribbon,** 98¢ per yard; **antique gold beads,** $4.98 each, *both from M&J Trimmings, 1008 Sixth Avenue, New York, NY 10018; 212-391-9072.*

pages 78, 80

Antique tassel, $37.98, *from M&J Trimmings, 1008 Sixth Avenue, New York, NY 10018; 212-391-9072.* 25"-long **mailing tube,** $2.95; single-weight **chipboard,** 72¢ each, *both from New York Central Art Supply, 62 Third Avenue, New York, NY 10003; 212-473-7705 or 800-950-6111 (outside NYC).* **Silk taffeta,** $42.95 per yard; *from B&J Fabrics, 263 West 40th Street, New York, NY 10018; 212-354-8212.*

pages 79, 80

Iridescent raw silk, $15.95 to $26.95 per yard, *from B&J Fabrics, 263 West 40th Street, New York, NY 10018; 212-354-8212.*

page 81

Cork, priced according to size, *from Milan Labs, 57 Spring Street, New York, NY 10012; 212-226-4780.*

page 82

½"-wide **copper tape,** $6.92 for 6 yards, *from Delphi Glass, 2116 East Michigan Avenue, Lansing, MI 48912; 517-482-2617 or 800-248-2048.* **Jax brass, bronze, and copper darkener,** $9 per pint, *from Metalliferous, 34 West 46th Street, New York, NY 10032; 212-944-0909*

page 83

Seashells, $25 for 20-pound bag of assorted colors and sizes ($20 minimum order), *at the Shell Man, P.O. Box 1917, Key Largo, FL 33037; 305-451-0767.* **Wooden frame** *by Green Mountain Studios Inc.,* $9 for 12" x 16", *at craft stores nationwide.* **Hemlock cones,** $10 for 6-ounce bag; red alder cones, $10 for 1-pound bag, *both from the Everyday Gardener, 2945 Old Canton Road, Jackson, MS 39216; 601-981-0273.* **Mat,** $25, *cut by Skyframe & Art Inc., 96 Spring Street, New York, NY 10012; 212-925-7856.* **Poplar frame,** $5, *from New York Central Framing, 102 Third Avenue, New York, NY 10003; 212-420-6060.*

page 84

Antique velvet, about $250 per yard, *from Cora Ginsburg, 19 East 74th Street, New York, NY 10021; 212-744-1352. By appointment.* **Chocolate-brown velvet,** $23.95 to $42.95 per yard, *from B & J Fabrics, 263 West 40th Street, New York, NY 10018; 212-354-8150.*

page 85

Wood-bottomed trays, *from houseware and Williams-Sonoma stores nationwide.* Pittsburgh Interior Enamel **paint, in avocado** (semigloss),

from $10.89 (quart) to $28.79 (gallon); **parchment** (eggshell finish), from $10.19 (quart) to $29.49 (gallon); *call 800-441-9695 for nearest retailer.* ⅞"-wide **satin ribbon,** $1.60 per yard, *at Hyman Hendler Inc., 67 West 38th Street, New York, NY 10018; 212-840-8393. Ribbons also from Britex Fabrics, 146 Geary Street,*

San Francisco, CA 94108; 415-392-2910.

page 86

White and black **artist's sketchbooks** by Cachet, $5.75 to $15.95, depending on size; Robert Simmons **stencil brush #96,** $2.30 to $4.05; Sobo **craft-and-fabric glue,** $1.85 for 4 ounces; *all from A.I. Friedman, 44 West 18th Street, New York, NY 10011; 212-243-9000. Minimum mail order $10. Also at art-supply stores.* Tina Vert (#4350/40) **green-and-white-stripe,** Milly Amethyst (#4354/71) **purple-check,** Milly Or (#4354/27) **yellow-check,** and La Musardière Jaune-Blanc (#11326/03) **yellow-print fabrics,** *all from Manuel Canovas, 979 Third Avenue, New York, NY 10022; 212-752-9588. To the trade only.* **Seersucker,** *at fabric stores nationwide.* **Linen,** price depends on width and weave, *from New York Central Art Supply, 62 Third Avenue, New York, NY 10003; 212-473-7705 or 800-950-6111 (outside NYC).* **Bone folder,** $3.50 for 6", $4.50 for 8", *both from New York Central Art Supply, see above.*

page 87

Kenized silver cloth, $9.95 per yard, *from B&J Fabrics, 263 West 40th Street, New York, NY 10018; 212-354-8150;* $18.99 per yard, *from Britex Fabrics, 146 Geary Street, San Francisco, CA 94108; 415-392-2910.* ¼" **midi braid** (#1703-WF), 10¢ per yard, *from Farber Braid*

Co., 48 West 38th Street, New York, NY 10018; 212-719-5820. Handmade **silver flatware,** about $850 per place setting, *from James Robinson, 480 Park Avenue, New York, NY 10022; 212-752-6166.* ⅝" **satin ribbon,** $1.30 per yard, and ⅜" **grosgrain ribbon,** $1.60 per yard, *both from Hyman Hendler & Sons, 67 West 38th Street, New York, NY 10018; 212-840-8393. Ribbons also from Britex Fabrics, see above.*

pages 88, 89

Weck Home Canning 1-liter **deco jar,** $14.95 for set of 4, *from Glashaus, 415 West Golf Road, Suite 13, Arlington Heights, IL 60005; 708-640-6918. Mail order only.*

page 89

Weck Home Canning 1-liter **tulip jar,** $16.25 for 6, *from Glashau, 415 West Golf Road, Suite 13, Arlington Heights, IL 60005; 708 640 6918. Mail order only.* **Sealing wax,** $3.50 per stick, *from Kate's Paperie, 8 West 13th Street, New York, NY 10011; 212-633-0570.*

page 90

Grosgrain ribbon, starting at $10 per yard for 4" to 6" widths, *from Hyman Hendler & Sons, 67 West 38th Street, New York, NY 10018; 212-840-8393. Ribbon also from Britex Fabrics, 146 Geary Street, San Francisco, CA 94108; 415-392-2910.* **5" gift boxes,** $5.25 each, *from Party Bazaar, Cross County Shopping Center, Yonkers, NY 10704; 914-965-1465.* **Sugar beads,** $1.89 for 4 ounces, *from New York Cake & Baking Center, 56 West 22nd Street, New York, NY 10010; 212-675-2253 or 800-942-2539.*

page 92

Parfait jars at kitchenware stores. 4" **Ball jars,** 95¢, *from Broadway Panhandler, 477 Broome Street, New York, NY 10013; 212-966-3434.*

page 93

2"-by-3" drawstring **muslin bags,** $1 for 5, and **potpourri supplies,** *available from Aphrodisia, 264 Bleecker Street, New York, NY 10014; 212-989-6440.*

CANDLES

pages 94, 96, 97

Beeswax sheets, 30¢ per inch for 8"-wide sheet or $5 per 8"-by-16" sheet, *from Bernard Roth, 9 Willow Street, Jersey City, NJ 07305; 201-432-4097.* **Natural beeswax,** $6.50 per pound, *available at Surma, 11 East 7th Street, New York, NY 10003; 212-477-0729.* **Wicking,** 60¢ per package, **paraffin,** about $1 per pound, **wick tabs** (for votives), 80¢ per package, and **dye pellets,** 65¢ each, *all from Barker*

Enterprise, 15106 10th Avenue SW, Seattle, WA 98116; 206-244-1870 or 800-543-0601.

page 97

Lead type, $15 per pound, *from M&H Type, 460 Bryant Street, San Francisco, CA 94107; 415-777-0716.*

pages 98, 99

Wax-pouring container, $11.75, and **thermometer,** $4.99, *both from Barker Enterprise, 15106 10th Avenue, SW, Seattle, WA 98116; 206-244-1870 or 800-543-0601.*

pages 100, 101

Bleached beeswax, $8.50 per pound, **wicking,** 79¢ for 8', **wick tabs,** 80¢ per package, and **assorted fragrance oils,** *all from Barker Enterprises, 15106 Tenth Avenue SW, Seattle, WA 98166; 206-244-1870 or 800-543-0601.* **Pure herbal oils,** $11 per ounce of lavender, $15 per ounce of sandalwood, $24 per ounce of jasmine, *from Aveda; 800-328-0849.* Antique Belgian **terra-cotta pots,** $9 to $26, *from L. Becker Flowers, 217 East 83rd Street, New York, NY 10028; 212-*

439-6001. **French flowerpots,** $1.25 each (minimum order of 12), *from Grass Roots Garden, 131 Spring Street, New York, NY 10012; 212-226-2662.* **Thumb pots,** $3.50 each (minimum order of 25), *from Timothy Mawson, Main Street, New Preston, CT 06777; 203-868-0732. Also at nurseries and garden-supply stores.* **Pure bees-wax,** $5 to $8 per pound; **cotton wick,** $3.50 for 10 yards, *both from E.A. Weiss & Co., 3 Whipstick Road, Wilton, CT 06897; 203-762-3538.*

pages 102, 103

Wicking, 79¢ per package, **paraffin,** about

$1 per pound, and **dye pellets,** 69¢ each, *all available from Barker Enterprise, 15106 10th Avenue SW, Seattle, WA 98116; 206-244-1870 or 800-543-0601.* **Natural beeswax,** $6.50 per pound, *at Surma, 11 East 7th Street, New York, NY 10003; 212-477-0729.* **Metal candle molds,** from $10, and **votive molds,** $1.75 each, *from Pourette Candle Co., 1419 NW 53rd Street, P.O. Box 17056, Seattle, WA 98107; 206-789-3188 or 800-888-9425.*

page 103

Candle sharpener, $1.25, *from Crate & Barrel stores nationwide.*

WRAPPING

page 104

Wire-edged taffeta ribbon, $1.50 to $11.50 per yard, *from Hyman Hendler & Sons, 67 West 38th Street, New York, NY 10018; 212-840-8393.* **Natural Nepal paper #5,** $2 per sheet; **antique rose Moriki paper #2008,** $6.45 per sheet, *both from New York Central Art Supply, 62 Third Avenue, New York, NY 10003; 212-473-7705 or 800-950-6111 (outside NYC).* **Neon-colored price tags** *from office-supply stores.*

page 105

Rice paper, priced according to pattern, *from Kate's Paperie, 561 Broadway, New York, NY 10012; 212-941-9816. Also at New York Central Art Supply, 62 Third Avenue, New York, NY 10003; 212-473-7705 or 800-950-6111 (outside NYC).* Antique metallic **ribbon,** $10-$25 per yard, *from Bell'occhio, 8 Brady Street, San Francisco, CA 94103; 415-864-4048.*

page 106

Special thanks to Lisa Bradkin at Takashimaya, 693 Fifth Avenue, New York, NY 10022; 800-228-1810.

page 107

Ribbons *from Britex Fabrics, 146 Geary Street, San Francisco, CA 94108; 415-392-2910.*

pages 108, 112, 114

Metallic tissue paper, $10 for 24 sheets in gold or silver, *from Party Bazaar, Cross County Shopping Center, Yonkers, NY 10704; 914-965-1465.*

page 109

5"-by-9" Kraft **papier-mâché boxes,** $6, *from Terra Verde, 120 Wooster Street, New York, NY 10012; 212-925-4533.* **Pale-yellow Lana Ingres paper,** 60¢ per sheet, *from New York Central Art Supply, 62 Third Avenue, New York, NY 10003; 212-473-7705 or 800-950-6111 (outside NYC).*

pages 109, 111

Paper ribbon, $3 per roll; *from Kate's Paperie, 8 West 13th Street, New York, NY 10011; 212-633-0570.*

page 110

Staedtler large **plastic eraser,** $2, *available at art-supply stores nationwide.* Small **sponge roller,** $2.75, *from New York Central Art Supply, 62 Third Avenue, New York, NY 10003; 212-473-7705 or 800-950-6111 (outside NYC).* **Japanese vegetable cutters,** $3.25 for set of 4; **cookie cutters,** 75¢ and up, *both from Broadway Panhandler, 477 Broome Street, New York, NY 10013; 212-966-3434.* **Olive Fabriano paper #709,** $1.57 per sheet, **brown Shalk paper,** $2.20 per sheet; **sea-green Moriki paper #2034,** $6.45 per sheet, *all from New York Central Art Supply, see above.* **Yellow French Kraft paper,** $5.95 per roll, *from Kate's Paperie, 8 West 13th Street, New York, NY 10011; 212-633-0570.*

page 111

Sealing wax, $3.50 per stick, *from Kate's Paperie, 8 West 13th Street, New York, NY 10011; 212-633-0570.* **Tissue paper** *by Crystal Tissue Co., available at party-goods stores nationwide.* **Neoprene tubing,** 36¢ to $1.39; **antivibration pad,** $1.60 to $9.40, *both from Canal Rubber Supply Co., 329 Canal Street, New York, NY 10013; 212-226-7339.* **Burgundy Moriki paper #2012,** $5.95 per sheet, *from New York Central Art Supply; 212-473-7705 or 800-950-6111 (outside NYC).*

page 112

Brown Shalk paper, $2.20 per sheet; **sea-green Moriki paper #2034,** $6.45 per sheet, *from New York Central Art Supply; 212-473-7705 or 800-950-6111 (outside NYC).* **Yellow French Kraft paper,** $5.95 per roll, *from Kate's Paperie, 561 Broadway, New York, NY 10012; 212-941-9816.* **Polka-dot ribbon,** $18 per yard, *from Bell'occhio, 8 Brady Street, San Francisco, CA 94103; 415-864-4048.* **Tracing vellum,** 50¢ per sheet, *from Pearl Paint Co., 308 Canal Street, New York, NY 10013; 212-431-7932. Catalogue $1; send address to Customer Service or call 800-221-6845.*

pages 113, 120

Silk buttonhole **thread** by Gütermann, $1.75 per spool, *from Greenberg & Hammer, 24 West 57th Street, New York, NY 10019; 212-246-2836.*

page 114

3"-by-2"-by-8" **cellophane bags,** $12.50 per 100, *from Melissa Neufeld Inc., 800-638-3353.*

Other sizes available. **Corrugated paper,** $4 for 31"-by-21" sheet, and **German waxed paper,** $2.50 for 28"-by-39" sheet, *both from Kate's Paperie, 8 West 13th Street, New York, NY 10011, 212-633-0570.*

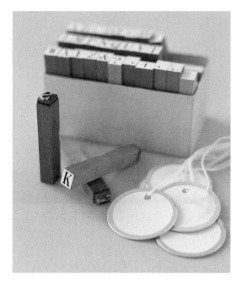

pages 114, 120
Cream-colored card stock, $2.28 for 10"-by-10" sheet, *from Pearl Paint Co., 308 Canal Street, New York, NY 10013; 212-431-7932. Catalogue $1; send address to Customer Service or call 800-221-6845.*

page 116
⅝" **satin ribbon,** $1.30 per yard, and ⅜" **grosgrain ribbon,** $1.60 per yard, *both from Hyman Hendler & Sons, 67 West 38th Street, New York, NY 10018; 212-840-8393. Ribbons also from Britex Fabrics, 146 Geary Street, San Francisco, CA 94108; 415-392-2910.*

page 117
Japanese mingei (patterned) **kozo paper,** $14 to $18 for 24"-by-36" sheet in contemporary patterns, $17 to $20 for variable sizes in vintage patterns, *available at New York Central Art Supply, 62 Third Avenue, New York, NY 10003; 212-473-7705 or 800-950-6111 (outside NYC). Japanese papers, from $3 to $24 per sheet, also from Flax, P.O. Box 7216, San Francisco, CA 94120-7216; 415-468-7530. Standard catalogue free, Collage catalogue $3; 800-926-5524.* **Stencils,** $19.99 for 12" capital alphabet, $7.99 for 6" capitals and numbers, *from New York Central Art Supply, see above.* **Raffia cord,** $15 for 144 yards, *from Tinsel Trading, 47 West 38th Street, New York 10018; 212-730-1030.* Crimson and taffeta **ribbons** *from Bell'occhio, 8 Brady Street, San Francisco, CA 94103; 415-864-*

4048. *Ribbons also from Britex Fabrics, 146 Geary Street, San Francisco, CA 94108; 415-392-2910.* **Escort cards and envelopes,** $25 for 50; **white note cards and envelopes,** $35 for 50, *both from Tiffany & Co., 727 Fifth Avenue, New York, NY 10022; 212-755-8000.* Custom-made **embosser,** from $30, *from Empire Stamp and Seal, 36 East 29th Street, New York, NY 10016; 212-679-5370.* **Wax stamps,** $16 to $24; **sealing wax,** $4 to $6 per stick, *both from Pearl Paint; 212-431-7932 or 800-221-6845.* **6"-by-6" envelopes,** $10.80 for 50, *from Paper Access; 800-727-3701.*

pages 117, 118
Aluminum tags, $1.19 to $1.30 for package of 6, *from Tanner-Durso Printing, 547 Broadway, New York, NY 10012; 212-226-0001.* **Stamp kits,** $35 for ¼" capital alphabet, *made to order from Rubber Stamps, 30 West 24th Street, New York, NY 10010, 212-675-1180. Kits of 1" letters, $12.16, also available from Pearl Paint Co., 308 Canal Street, New York, NY 10013; 212-431-7932. Catalogue $1; send address to Customer Service or call 800-221-6845.*

page 119
Sennelier iridescent transparent **oil pastels,** $2.06 each, *from Pearl Paint Co., 308 Canal Street, New York, NY 10013; 212-431-7932. Catalogue $1; send address to Customer Service or call 800-221-6845.*

pages 120
6"-by-6" envelopes, $10.80 for 50, *from Paper Access; 800-727-3701.* **Wooden alphabet stamps,** $25 to $180, *from Stampa Barbara, 505 Paseo Nuevo, Santa Barbara, CA 93101; 805-962-4077.* **Color Aid paper,** $41.40 for 220 6"-by-9" sheets (includes several colors), *from New York Central Art Supply; 62 Third Avenue, New York, NY 10003 212-473-7705 or 800-950-6111 (outside NYC).* **Glassine envelopes,** *from Adorama, 42 West 18th Street, New York, NY 10011; 212-741-0052.*

page 121
Glassine envelopes, $2 to $5.75 for pack of 100, depending on size, *at Stampazine, 119 West 57th Street, New York, NY 10019; 212-262-0100.* **2"-by-2" glassine envelopes,** $6.95 for 100, *at Adorama, 42 West 18th Street, New York, NY 10011; 212-741-0052 or 800-223-2500.* **42"-by-100' rolls of glassine,** $60.25, *at Talas, 568 Broadway, New York, NY 10012; 212-219-0770.* **Glassine envelopes, sheets, and rolls** *also from University Products; 800-628-1912. Free catalogue.*

THE GREAT OUTDOORS
Greenery also available at local Christmas-tree sellers.

pages 123, 125
Grapevine balls, $15.95, $21.95, and $31.95, depending on size, *available from Joe Makrancy's Garden and Floral Shop, 966 Kuser Road, Trenton, NJ 08619; 609-587-2543. Grapevine, forms, and lights for do-it-yourself also available.*
Transparent Venetian minilights, $15 for 100-light 50' cord, *from Just Bulbs, 936 Broadway, New York, NY 10010; 212-228-7820 or 800-544-4877.*

page 124
On arbor: **stars on a string,** $20 for 10 stars, *all from Just Bulbs, 936 Broadway at East 22nd Street, New York, NY 10010; 212-228-7820 or 800-544-4877.* On lamppost: **C-7 white solid and clear bulbs,** $10 for 15-light 15' cord, *all from Just Bulbs, 936 Broadway at East 22nd Street, New York, NY 10010; 212-228-7820 or 800-544-4877.*

pages 125, 126
C-9 clear and white, $25 for 25-light 25' cord, **C-9 multicolor solid,** $25 for 25-light 25' cord, **clear Venetian minilights,** $7.50 for 50-light 23' cord; **10G/12½K clear golf-ball multicolor bulbs** (on wreath), $1.50 each; **C-9 solid color bulbs,** $25 for 25-light 25' cord, *all from Just Bulbs, 936 Broadway at East 22nd Street, New York, NY 10010; 212-228-7820 or 800-544-4877.*

page 127 to 133
Florist's wire on paddle, $1.59 for 22-gauge, $1.98 for 26-gauge, *both from Dorothy Biddle Service, HC01 Box 900, Greeley, PA 18425; 717-226-3239.*

INDEX

If you have enjoyed reading and
using *The Best of Martha Stewart Living:
Handmade Christmas* please join us as
a subscriber to Martha Stewart Living,
the magazine. Call toll-free 800-999-6518.
The annual subscription rate is
$24 for 10 issues.